PET MOMENTS.

BY

R. A. DOUGLAS-LITHGOW.

" I look
Not without gentle sadness upon thee,
And liken thy outgoing, O, my book,
To the impatience of a little brook,
Which might with flowers have lingered pleasantly,
Yet toils to perish in the mighty sea."
Archbishop Trench.

" Be it with thee according to thy worth,
Go, little book! in faith I send thee forth."
Southey.

LONDON:
PROVOST & CO., 36, HENRIETTA STREET,
COVENT GARDEN.

1877.

PRINTED FOR

PROVOST AND CO., 36, HENRIETTA STREET,
COVENT GARDEN.

CONTENTS.

———◦◦———

PREFACE.

THE majority of those who publish begin by saying that a preface is unnecessary; then they write one; and, finally, they apologise for doing so. For my own part, I never read a book without first perusing such prefatory remarks as there may be; and I think it reasonable that the public,—for whom most publications are intended, — should have some introduction to the author, and, if a personal one, so much the better. Of course this only applies to those who are unknown as authors, and especially to those who have rashly rushed into print for the first time: but a few words of introduction are, I believe, calculated to promote a better understanding between author and reader, and may, in some measure, atone for the shortcomings of the one, while they appeal to the sympathies and forbearance of the other.

The author of this little book of rhymes has

B

always found his greatest enjoyment in literary
pursuits of some kind or other; and, in hours of
fatigue and depression such as come to all, he
has ever found rest and solace amongst the Muses.
The poetic trifles in this volume are the result of
" pet moments" spent in their society, and are
now collected and published in deference to the
oft-repeated solicitations of many friends who, the
writer has every reason to believe, will welcome
and appreciate them still more in their present
collective form.

Written, as they have been, in the intervals of
study and of active professional work,—at all
hours of the night and day, and often under most
romantic circumstances,—they should disarm criti-
cism, as the smile of a child might disarm a frowning warrior.

The North Brink,
Wisbech, Cambs.

PET MOMENTS.

TO ALFRED TENNYSON.

To thee, around whose genius-lighted brow
A nation's hands have bound the laureate wreath,—
Whose honoured name with loving pride is shrined
Deep in the chambers of the people's hearts ;—
Whose mighty mind has deftly, subtly, wrought
A web of king-thoughts destined to endure,
And glow undimmed, untarnished through all
    time ;—
Whose noble heart, throbbing with soul-fed springs
Of love and sympathy for all mankind,
Hath moved thee to unbar the golden gates
Of genial Fancy, setting free her light
To tint and mellow that diviner gleam
Which pours its radiance round immortal Truth,—
To wile the sunshine from Life's fleeting hours,
And spread it o'er the paths of Right and Worth ;—
Whose gentle soul beams like a lover's eyes

O'er every genius-written, tuneful page,
Begetting kindred love for all that's pure,
And true, and beautiful; begetting hate
For rank hypocrisy, and heartless pride,
For foul injustice, cowardice, and crime :—
To thee a youthful rhymer would present
A bouquet formed of simple, wilding flowers,
Gathered in leisure moments, here and there,
Along the busy road of daily life ;
A humble tribute to thy gifted mind,
A token of unfeignèd gratitude
From one whom thou hast honoured, and to whom
Thy kindly hand hath written words of joy.
May health be thine, through many happy years,
And every blessing crown thy worthy life ;
May love encompass thee, and consecrate
Thy heart's desires,—the yearnings of thy soul,
With joys perennial, and eternal peace.
Thy country's honour, and the people's pride,—
The conquests of thy genius still revered,—
May time but add fresh honour to thy bays,
And sanctify thy spirit with pure joy :
And, o'er that scroll whereon proud Fame records
The noble worth of Britons, great and good,
May TENNYSON's loved name for ever gleam !

AN ASPIRATION.

Oh! would I had a poet's soul—
A poet's power—a poet's pen,
How I would strive in brotherhood
To federalise my fellow-men!
I'd have the rich to help the poor,
The poor to trust the great;
I'd have all men combined in love,
Whatever their estate.

In unison the people's hearts
Would glow with fervent zeal;
And Love and Truth maintain the Right
In Freedom's Commonweal:
Nor fear, nor pride, would mar the sway
Which Right exerts o'er Wrong;
The weak in confidence would cling
For succour to the strong.

No law would favour sect or race
To suit or class or creed;
No gentle blood, or tinselled rank,
On honest worth would feed.

But fearless Justice would go forth
Inflexible o'er earth;
And every germ of tyranny
Be strangled in its birth.

No more would Superstition's reins
Direct the nation's mind;
No more would stubborn Prejudice
The wings of Conscience bind;
But Freedom's powerful arm would crush
Each coward tyrant's rod;
And souls, untrammelled, would commune
Devoutly with their God.

The sheen of Truth would brightly gleam
O'er earth's benignant face,
And conscience-gifted men would *think*
And *act* to serve their race.
Mankind, beatified and free,
Exalted, noble, good,
Would merit gracious Heaven's smile,
And live in brotherhood!

I'd liberate man's mighty mind,
And guide it in its flight,
Till Virtue's strength would aid its wings
To soar in Wisdom's light.

And high and low, and rich and poor,
Would bathe in Truth's deep tide,
Till man regenerate became,
And Heaven glorified!

Oh! for the power—the mighty power—
To lead the hearts of men;
The poet's noble soul to guide
The poet's powerful pen!
Oh! for the time—the happy time—
When Might must yield to Worth;
When Freedom, Truth, and Love shall reign
And flourish upon earth!

LOVE-LINKS.

GOLDEN hair o'er mild blue eyes,
Golden dreams in Love's fair dawn,
Golden beams o'er soft blue skies,
Golden hopes—alas! all gone—
Yet linger they as memories.

Golden smiles o'er sweet blue flowers,
Gathered in Love's golden spring,
Blue-bells wet with tearful showers,
Faded flowers—a broken ring—
Souvenirs of golden hours!

THE MINISTRY OF NATURE.

"Farewell, cold world, farewell ! I flee to thee,
O Nature ! Hail thou solitary Vale !
And hither come, Imagination ! Come,
And waft my soul to isles of poesy !"

ᴇʙᴇɴᴇᴢᴇʀ ᴇʟʟɪᴏᴛ.

"There is a lesson in each flower,
A story in each stream and bower ;
In every herb on which you tread
Are written words which, rightly read,
Will lead you from earth's fragrant sod,
To hope, and holiness, and God."

ᴀʟʟᴀɴ ᴄᴜɴɴɪɴɢʜᴀᴍ.

NESTLED beside the heart of dear old England,
The haunt of rustic elf and guardian gnome,
A leafy lane lies bosomed in a valley
Which owns no rival in our island-home.
Here, from the hamlet but a short mile westward,
Often I steal, with poet's ardour moved,
To wing, in solitude, imagination,
And drink from Fancy's chalice unreproved.
Hither, one summer day, I sadly wandered,
Pining that Life would cede no happy chance

To realise youth's day-dreams in my manhood,—
By contrariety of circumstance
Locked, spell-bound, in the backward, dreary distance
Which I had travelled,—whence I first essayed
To run the gauntlet through earth's moil and
    warfare,
Nor paused to note the progress I had made. ·
Chafing with mental weariness and languor,
My drooping spirit lone and anguish-fraught,
I threw myself upon the daisied clover,
A writhing martyr on the rack of thought.
Nor long I lay before, like magic essence ·
Which subtle alchemists of yore distilled,
I felt a mystic-breath around me glowing,
And mystic whispers through my being thrilled.
Meseemed to feel the touch of holy angels
Quicken the current of my spirit's flow,
And music, sweet as from a choir of seraphs,—
Rapture I thought no mortal e'er could know,—
Entered my soul; the echoing vibrations
Trembling with bliss, intensified, supreme,
Through the ecstatic flood which swelled my bosom,
Like sunbeams dancing o'er a crystal stream.
Methought mankind had disappeared for ever,
Man and his works had faded from the earth,
That I, alone, henceforth must live and wander

Where mankind dwelt not :—where nor death, nor
    birth,
Or sorrow's wail, or parents' acclamation
Would break my isolated solitude,—
And occupy the world like a lone pilgrim
Threading the mazes of a tangled wood,
Whose waving depths, and labyrinths primeval
The alien foot of man had never trod ;
Alone ! myself humanity embodied,
Alone ! with Nature, and with Nature's GOD !
Nor was my soul unhappy, for around me
Wafted the perfume of Elysian bowers,
And peace, and love, and innocence enhallowed
A paradise of verdure and sweet flowers,
Where Melody reëchoed o'er the mountains,
Flooding the valleys with her dulcet swell,
And balmy zephyrs wooed eternal sunshine,
Breathing enchantment o'er each flowery dell.
No trace of sin, no frowning cloud of evil
Darkened the flowery sod or azure sky,
But, in a world of Eden's pristine beauty
Truth's sheen illumed Love's immortality.
Knelt I in humble and sincere devotion,
Breathing the fervour which my soul possessed,
Until, exhausted by ecstatic passion,
Swooning, I sank upon fond Nature's breast.

Glowed then a holy calm within my bosom,
And whispers soft, as if from angels near
Floated like liquid music through the ether,
And smote with rapture on my ravished ear.
Seemed to arise before me a fair spirit,
Bright as the halo o'er the brow of morn,
Beaming her smile as aureate clouds at sunset,—
Radiance divine, and beauty heaven-born
Shedding a sacred lustre round her presence,
Gemming the azure of her dewy eyes,
From which outshone a gleam of holy love-light,
Soft as the golden sheen of summer skies.
Then she:
    " Come hither, oh beloved mortal!
" With joy I greet thee in thy solitude."
Then I arose in trembling adoration,
And prostrate fell before her, love-subdued.
" Nay worship none but God alone, our Father!
" Arise!   And listen to the voice of Love ;
" Fulfil the noble mission here assigned thee,
" Then share the mansions of thy Lord above,
" With simple faith, and uniform obedience,
" The path of duty follow undismayed ;
" Study thy life-chart by the light of conscience,
" And upward, onward, of no toil afraid,—
" Scorning impossibilities and danger,

" And, ever buoyed by humble, earnest trust,—
" Press to the goal with ceaseless, bold endeavour,
" Trample self-yearnings in the abject dust :
" Nourish despair by no debased inaction,
" But through Life's pilgrimage, determined, plod,
" And, in a heart of hallowed aim and purpose,
" Cherish the Right, and do it ; trust in God ! "
Thus having said, she smiled, and pointed upward,
And,—like the waves of Fancy's golden light
Which gild the domes and palaces of dreamland
When Reason sleeps,—evanished from my sight,
Just as the transient galaxies of Fancy
Fade into nothingness when Reason wakes,
To re-ascend her throne ; and, with her sceptre,
The subtle spell of the usurper breaks.

As rosy Morning steals Night's sable mantle
From sleeping Nature's dew-bespangled breast,
So sped the fleeting charms which lulled my
        senses,—
Perished the vision which my soul caressed :—
And I, with happy, but bewildered spirit,—
While ransomed Thought with wayward Fancy
        strove,—
Awoke, reclining on the daisied clover
Which decks the haunt wherein I joy to rove.

Yes ! there are those who scorn the poet's numbers,
His loftiest flights regard as idle dreams,
Whose minds—the reflex of self-leavened natures—
Find naught but folly in his noblest themes.
Well, let them scoff! the bard reveres his mission
As holy, and beyond their envious rage ;
His numbers may be weak, yet ' point a moral '
To cheer some brother through Life's pilgrimage.
Thus : though I slept, and, dreaming, saw a vision
Which taught my soul a purer, holier creed
Than I had known before ;—(for dreams may teach
        us ;
Is there not honey in the vulgar weed ?)
I rose refreshed, and with a joyous spirit
Sauntered on pensively, and, save mine own,·
Nor other shade of mortal blurred the landscape ;
Before, behind, around, I was alone !
With pregnant calm of solitude within me,
Flashed through the courts of Memory the sheen
Of wingèd thoughts,—the phantoms of my day-
        dream,
Flushing with bliss what I had heard and seen :
Then, like a streamlet hasting to the river,—
A river bounding to the mighty sea,—
Now glided stealthily, then rushed sublimely,
Fresh soul-fed streams of glancing thought, set free

From hidden sources, by a mystic Agent
Who formed new channels for their even flow
Within my mind ; and, as the blush of virtue
Steals o'er the maiden's cheek, with love aglow,
When first her trembling bosom woos the rapture
Of love requited ; so upon me dawned
The hallowed teaching of my noon-day vision,
When Fancy touched me with her magic wand.
Be this my text ; though trite and unromantic,
Yet pure its doctrine, grave the message sent,
And plainly writ in Love's unerring symbols,
On Truth's fair page, by the Omnipotent !

Each trembling leaf, the zephyr, and the stream-
    let,—
Each flower which blooms upon the verdant sod,—
The roar of ocean, and the howl of tempest,
Speaks to the souls of men with voice from God !
There's not a tone, a touch, a look of Nature,
But tells of Him who gave her wonders birth ;
There's not a creature of all things created,—
In ocean's depths, upon the face of earth,—
But serves the purpose of the Great Creator,
Fulfilling wondrously His love-wrought plan,
Save him with mighty mind, a soul immortal,
And form most God-like,—unbelieving Man !

Oh ! that the sermons ever preached around us,
With all the melting eloquence of Love,—
By thousand voices of adoring Nature,
From sea, and fell, and mountain, dale and grove,—
Would touch with living fire the crumbling altars
Of poor humanity, and roll a flood
Of mighty Truth to overspread the nations,
Till men were sanctified in brotherhood.
Oh ! that the heralds of revealed religion
Would foster Nature's sermons more, and woo
Immortal souls, with cadences as gentle
As lover's words, in rapture stealing through
Love's rosy gate, when passion-woke vibrations,
Trembling around Affection's harp, give birth
To those emotions which, upborne by Virtue,
And taught Love's own sweet language, issue forth,
Wafting the music of the soul in numbers
Which charm the silence of the moon's soft light,
Like the sweet nightingale's melodious solo,
Thrilling the bosom of enchanted Night.
Not with a sneer of sanctity superior,
Nor with the dogmas of a stunted creed ;
Not with the sacerdotal superstitions
Which on the ignorance of mortals feed :
With no ecclesiastical vain-glory,
No base self-righteousness, unsanctified,

No broken chain of mythical succession,
No hollow cant, no Pharisaic pride ;
But on the vantage-ground of Life Eternal,
Where Truth's fair standard proudly waves un-
    furled,
With Love's soft touch, in tones of offered mercy,
Attune the heart-strings of an outlawed world.
Oh ye who minister in things most sacred,
Professing still these holy truths to teach,
Try not to warp explicit revelation,
Nor try to grasp what lies beyond thy reach,
Proclaim abroad the evangelic tidings
Of Love's intensity, and Mercy's flood,—
Salvation free and full for every creature
Whose faith is centred in a Saviour's blood !
The heaven-hallowed ministry of Nature,
Unerring, eloquent, devout, sublime,
Calls upon men to centre their affections
Beyond the phantasies of sense and time ;
To kneel upon the altar of earth's bosom,
And waft Faith's incense to the heights of Love,
Fraught with the soul's most sacred aspirations
To hold communion with her God above.
Between mankind and the Supreme Eternal
There is no fellowship—no way but one !
One Great High Priest—one Holy Mediator—

Man's only Saviour, GOD's Eternal Son:
Faith in the sacrifice of our Redeemer,—
Once offered up, for each loved soul, for all,—
Can pierce the blackest clouds of human darkness ;
Can rend asunder Evil's gloomy pall—
The sable drapery which hangs o'er mortals,
Casting the shadows of its baneful gloom
Over the glow of their immortal spirits,
Shrouding divineness in a living tomb.
Faith is the lamp which gleams from earth to heaven,
Illumining the Truth, the Life, the Way;
Pouring its radiance o'er the Christian's guerdon,—
The Crown of Love, in God's Eternity !

Lives there a soul who has not felt the sunshine
Of blissful rapture glowing through her shrine,—
Beats there a heart whose life-wave does not mantle
The god-like impress on "the face divine":—
When earth reëchoes with the hymn of Nature
Mounting on zephyrs' wings, and upward borne
Through the clear ether redolent with perfume—
Canopied over by the smile of Morn !
Lives there a soul unthrilled by Nature's teaching,
Beats there a heart which does not own her power,
And hear her sermons preached by every streamlet,
From every tree—from every leaf and flower?

c

Oh! Gentle Monitress! Benignant Nature!
By Truth's inviolable power direct
The springs of thought which animate men's actions,
And feed their minds.   The narrow-minded sect,
The selfish bigot, and the priestly tyrant,—
The canting hypocrite, and error's slave,—
The parasites of baneful superstition,—
And those whom ignorance and vice deprave,—
Subdue, and soften by thy hallowed teaching,
And through the darkness of their being move
The Spirit of the Gospel in its fulness,—
The God of Nature reigneth: "God is Love!"

Come forth, oh Sceptic!   Lo, the sun has risen,
And morning smiles upon the waking earth;
Hark! how the tuneful choristers of Nature
Herald the advent of the young day's birth!
The shades of night have vanished o'er the moun-
          tains,
The sun has flecked with gold the eastern hills,
Laden the zephyrs with the breath of flowers,
And gemmed the bosoms of the sportive rills.
Like unpent, penitential tears upwelling
From a poor sin-bound heart when touched by Love—
The dews ascend in clouds of fragrant incense,
Pearling the azure vault of heaven above.

Come! Let us ramble through the fields together,
And share the beauty of Aurora's smile,
Gleaming adown the bosom of the valley—
Glinting its radiance through each leafy aisle.
See! at our very feet, with joyous motion,
The tuneful lark from out her nest uprise,
Cleaving the air with trills of sweetest music—
Bearing her grateful anthem to the skies.
The cowslips and the daisies deck the meadows,
And every floweret wafts its fragrance round,
The streamlets murmur their refrain of gladness—
The leaf-clad trees with melody resound:
Look where you may, the soul of Life and Beauty
Touches the heart, and charms each waking sense,
While at the gates of Morn the suite of Nature
Worships and glorifies Omnipotence!
Nay, let us linger! through the purple orient
The day-god's golden chariot ascends
The pearly eminence of azure heaven,
And, zenith-ward careering, softly blends
The bright effulgence of its aureate splendour
With the soft-tinted amethystine hues
Yet lingering adown the east, and flushes
The face of Nature; while the balmy dews,
Rising behind the mighty sun-kissed mountains
Melt in the glowing, fragrant noontide air,

And joyous song-birds through the cloudless welkin
Pour forth their sweetest love-notes everywhere.
And now behold the monarch in his glory,
In regal pomp and sovereign array !
Hark ! how the hills and dales with joy reēcho,
When lovely Nature greets the King of Day !
The dreamy languors of the golden noontide
Float in the dalliance of the perfumed breeze,
The parti-coloured butterflies, disporting,
Flit through the sunshine ; while the hum of bees,
The chirp of grasshoppers, and whirring rustle
Of gauze-winged dragons, and pied ladybirds,
Reanimate the sultry, swooning zephyrs ;
And, in the floweryĮmeads, the lowing herds
Of drowsy cattle seek the leafy shelter
Of hedge-rows white with may, beneath whose
        shade,—
Clear as its crystal source within the mountain,—
A babbling brooklet, sparkling through the glade,
Winds like a thread of silver through the meadows,
Where many a wilding blossoms on its brink,
And where, betimes, it spreads its limpid waters
In glancing fords where panting kine may drink.
Though beautiful are Fancy's phantom visions,
The noon-day smile of Nature is more fair,
And, like her voice's soul-impassioned music,

Gladdens the earth, and lingers everywhere.
Oh, doubting one! give ear to Nature's teaching,
And let her hallowed light illume thy mind ;
Why pine and languish in chaotic darkness,
Alike to reason and to wisdom blind ?
Thy spirit is divinity embodied,
Therefore immortal; and, though Error's gloom,
Intensified by Sin's Avernian denseness,—
Thick with the murky brood from Evil's womb,
Oppress her wings : though poison-laden tendrils
Of Ignorance and Prejudice o'ergrow
The narrow confines of her prison-chamber,—
Dimming the lustre of her sacred glow,—
Yet, in the sempiternity of Being
She must exist ; either as Satan-bound
And sin-polluted here ;—(then doomed hereafter
To share that perpetuity, where sound
Of woe's despairing wail unutterable,
Reëchoes evermore :)—or shrined on earth
Within a bosom sanctified by mercy,
Where Love has consecrated Wisdom's birth;—
She basks beneath the smile of her Creator,—
Swayed by His mystic but supreme control,
And holds communion with the God of Spirits,—
Jehovah, Lord, the Universal Soul !—
Until, her discipline on earth being ended,—

Taking her flight across the sea of Death,
Beyond whose stream seraphic hosts await her,
While holy Faith her way illumineth,—
She mounts above the dark Lethean shadows,—
Beyond the nether mists of earth and sky,
And soars within the mysteries of Heaven,
To praise her God in Love's Eternity!
Oh, faithless one! Awake to Nature's teaching;
Thy doubtful mind is veilèd by a shroud
Of woeful woof; and, narcotised by evil,
Thy reason slumbers in a sombre cloud
Of direful ignorance.   Oh! burst the fetters
Which demon-hands have round thy being wove;
From Nature's book derive unerring wisdom,
And learn her sweet evangel,—" God is Love ! "
See now the sun, horizon-ward descending,
Incarnadines the bosom of the west;
Around his royal brow a purple halo,—
A gleam of splendour o'er his sovereign breast,
Whose sheen irradiates the western heavens,
And, from the monarch's diadem is rolled
Adown the arching dome, a flood of glory,—
Azure and crimson blent with molten gold.
Behold, again! the empyrean lustre
Has deepened into mellow, purple shades,
And pensive Eventide, with gentle footsteps

Each shrine of Nature timidly invades.
Her dewy breath embalms the drooping flowerets,
The zephyrs rest, the feathered songsters sleep,
The cloudlets darkle o'er her fleecy mantle,
While mist-veiled shadows from her bosom creep;—
And then, dissolving in tenebrious vapours,
Mellow with sepia tints the dappled sky,—
Deepen the glimmer of the halcyon twilight,
Sacred to Solitude and Memory.
Now gentle Hesperus, serenely beaming,
O'er resting Nature sheds her placid light,
And, one by one, the starry hosts assemble
To pay their homage to the queen of Night.
Behold, she comes ! the pearly-bosomed monarch
Before whom poets, saints, and lovers bow,
Upborne by silver clouds across the heavens,
A sacred halo round her virgin brow :
The dazzling reflex of her queenly beauty,
Night's gloomy veil with silver beams has rent,
And, like a courtier train on her attendant,
The blazing sapphires of the firmament
Exult in loyalty and love, yet tremble
Before her transcendental majesty ;
Her chaste sweet smile illumining the welkin,—
Flushing the earth with liquid argentry.
Now silence reigns ; enhallowed, universal,

No sound upon the wakeful ear intrudes,
Save lonely Philomel's melodious trilling,—
The laureate poet of the moon-lit woods.   ·
Oh ! let the holy influences stealing
Like gleams of heaven o'er Night's sable wings—
Freighting each pencil of the sacred moonlight,
(Pregnant with bliss and spirit-communings),
Hallow the subtle essence of thy being,
And fill the darkened chambers of thy soul
With Truth's eternal light : while Love inspireth
Thy new-born faith, and o'er thy spirit roll
The glorious, golden waves of Mercy's sunshine :
Oh ! while all Nature pleads, and angels wait,
While Virtue strives, and fettered Reason prays,
Acknowledge God with heart-regenerate.
Here, as the moonlight gleams o'er Earth's fair
      altar,
Bow down thy knee upon the verdant sod :
While Conscience cries in thunder-tones, " Repent
      thou,"
Believe, confess, and know *there is a* GOD !

And thou, too, cold Materialist ! Go ponder
The mystic lore in every varied page
Of Nature's hallowed book ! Go, find a witness,
At every footstep through Life's pilgrimage,

To the Supreme, Omnipotent Creator,
Spirit of Life, Eternal! At Whose word
A thousand worlds leaped from the womb of chaos,
And Time began: Whose sovereign fiat stirred
From depths abysmal, the unfathomed ocean
And meted out its boundaries; by Whom
Was said, "Let there be light!" and light abounded—
Flooding the vastness of primeval gloom:
Who formed this lovely earth, and framed the
        heavens,
Founded, and fixed in their appointed place
The pillars of the Universe:—suspended
Revolving systems in unbounded space,
And, when Creation teemed with Life and Beauty,
To crown the wonders of His love-wrought plan,
Moulded from clay, and fashioned in His image,
Creation's Steward,—His arch-creature, Man!
Go forth into the woodlands and the meadows,
And see the sun-flecked azure arching o'er
The beauteous landscape; hear the song-birds carol,
Or bend thy footsteps to the lone sea-shore:
Perceive in every leaf, and shell, and floweret
The mystic impress of a Great First Cause,
And worship thou the all-pervading Spirit
Who governs Nature by unerring laws.
Oh! contemplate the harmonies of Nature,

The countless evidences of Design,
The *means* to certain *ends; effects* of *causes,*
And agencies unnumbered, which combine
To testify through Truth's immortal medium,
Of that Omnipotent, Supreme Control
Directing Nature ;—Nature's Great Creator,
Eternal God,—the Universal Soul !
The living world within a drop of water,—
Each leaf that trembles on its parent tree,—
An insect's wing,—the simplest wilding blossom,—
Attests the holy seal of Deity !
Oh ! tear the veil, then, from thine erring reason,
And study Nature in her every mood ;
Go, trace the Maker's hand throughout Creation,
And testify to Love's infinitude !

Oh, happy they who with unfeignèd rapture
Can look on Nature with a lover's eyes,
And recognise in her protean aspects,
The earthly meed of Heaven's mysteries !
Who see in forest, valley, flood, and mountain,
In heaven's gold and azure sky above,
In flowers, and fruit, and trees ; in shade and sun-
    shine,
Creation's records of Eternal Love !
To whom the howling storm and gentle zephyr,
The sun by day, the moon and stars by night,

The silver streamlet, and the seething ocean,
Speak of a power Divine and Infinite !
Whose souls commune with the mysterious spirit
Pervading Nature ; and, through Faith, ascend
Beyond the nether earth and Time's horizon,
Where angel hosts with blissful joy attend
At Heaven's gates, to breathe their aspirations
As clouds of incense to the golden throne
Of Love Supreme : whither no cry for mercy,
No weary prodigal's repentant moan
E'er mounts in vain ; but, seraph-wafted, enters
The glorious courts of the Eternal King,
Who hears and answers evermore ; "Our Father,"
Whose Holy Will delights in pardoning.
Thus, from His footstool, whence adoring Nature
Worships her God, and swells her hymn of praise,
The thirsty pilgrim, and the wrestling sinner,
On wings of Faith their drooping souls may raise
Before the very mercy-seat of Heaven,
Where thirst is quenched in ever-flowing streams
Of boundless grace ; and through each sin-draped
        spirit
The hallowed sheen of Life Eternal gleams.
Thus soars the victor-christian's song of triumph,
The pleading heart-notes of the sin-defiled,—
Despair's wild shriek, — the fear-throbs of the
        tempted,—

The lisping accents of a praying child !
Hark, doubting brother ! to the myriad voices
Attesting Deity ! Around, abroad,
Through lovely Nature's consecrated temple,
At every footstep see the seal of God !
Come, hypocrite, materialist, self-righteous,
And thou, too, heartless, selfish one, come all !
Come, hardened sinner ! Come, thou weak and
    tempted, .
And from earth's bosom on her Maker call !
Oh, come ! And on the tablets of Creation
The great Creator's loving message trace,
Come, see the boundless fulness of His mercy,
Come, taste the endless rivers of His grace !
With Nature's choir exult, and hold communion
With Nature's God ; her hallowed converse share ;
From earth to Heaven angels soar and beckon,
And Love's own voice proclaims God everywhere !
Though veils of error mantle o'er thy reason,
And Life's rude way be cold, and drear, and dark,
Angels of Life and Love are ever round thee,—
(As saw the ancient Jewish Patriarch
Ascend, and then descend from earth to heaven :)—
And God is yearning with a Father's love,
To welcome back His erring, wayward children,
And with them share His glorious courts above !

WHITE CONVOLVULUS.

(*Convolvulus Sepium*)

THERE is a simple wildflower which ever wafts a spell
Around Affection's ruin in this saddened heart of
mine,
Like the mystic breath of Naiads in some fairy wood-
land dell,
Or the whisperings of angels through a desolated
shrine.

Oh! tenderly and well I love my humble little flower,
As pure and chastely beautiful as aught I know on
earth,
With modest comeliness surpassing all in Flora's
bower,
Yet blooming but to perish on the day which gave it
birth.

In native grace and meekness, oh! sadly dear to me,
Is hawthorn-breathed Convolvulus which decks the
sweet hedgerow,
And never in its fragrant haunt the pallid bloom I
see,
But soul-shrined recollections wake the happy
long-ago.

Long-cherished, sacred memories within its bosom
 sleep,
Which thrill with soft emotion through my sorrow-
 stricken soul,—
As re-animating sunbeams o'er the dew-wet flowerets creep,
And, o'er the tear-stained brow of Morn, a flood of
 perfume roll.

Its tendrils twine a love-knot on the woodbine and
 the may,
And round the wooing blossoms with their lily-
 chaplet run,—
Like Affection's spring-time blending lovers' hearts
 in ecstasy :—
So perfumes blend,—so lovers' souls are merged in
 unison.

Oh ! oft with white Convolvulus, a floral crown I
 wove
To deck the auburn ringlets on my darling's snow-
 white brow,
When, with Summer's smile around us, and a
 Summer sky above,
Soft zephyrs sped to Heaven with each consecrated
 vow.

The fairest flowers must wither, and the ' form
    divine ' must fade,
Yet Spring will smile hereafter, and the soul can
    never die;
So ruthless Death may show to Time the changes
    he has made,
But Time and Death are swallowed up in Immor-
    tality!

Though years have fled since angels bore my loved
    one to her rest,—
Though Love's sweet spell is broken, and my life
    is overcast,
Yet the little flower she loved has still the power to
    charm my breast,
Recalling youth's Elysium in the dreamland of the
    past.

Convolvulus! Fair emblem thou of beauty's sad
    decay,
At morn,—at noon, a lovely flower,—blighted at
    eventide;
Thy short-lived blossoming proclaims the flight of
    Life's brief day,
And tells how swiftly from his grasp, Time's soul-
    fraught moments glide.

Oh, yes ! I love thy gentle form, meek wildling as
    thou art,
Thou speakest of my sainted one, "not lost, but
    gone before,"
And while life's sand keeps flowing, I shall prize
    thee in my heart,
And only cease to cherish thee when I shall be no
    more !

ONE LITTLE GOLDEN HOUR.

I GAZE adown the vista of the Past ;—
The many-coloured, thought-inspiring Past,
Where reigneth Memory, 'mid sepia tints,
And gleams of sunshine : toward the portal speeds
A motley crowd of phantom wayfarers,
Whose forms, albeit but aërial,
Deepen in outline as they, thronging, pour
From out the dim perspective : on they rush,
And ever on, in number infinite,
Peopling the mazes of Mnemosyne ;—
The fleeting vanguard of the long-ago,
Pursuing close the stealthy-footed Now !
One little golden Hour of recent birth,
Yet fondly clasped in Memory's soft embrace,

Smiles on the bosom of its fostering nurse,
And fills the sacred chamber with delight.
Beauty has stamped her royal impress on
The infant's brow: and Hope, and Truth, and
        Peace,
With gentle hands caress the darling child,
While joyous Love imprints upon its cheek,
With glowing fervour, an impassioned kiss.
I gaze enraptured on the charming scene,
And, as the sheen of memory gleameth round
The living picture, burns within my soul
An impulse irresistible; and springs
Within my heart a stream of pure delight,
Which fills my being with the thoughts of song,
And, thus elated, I essay to sing.

———

We met in a festive throng,
        Phillis and I,
And charmed by the joys of dance and song,
Old Time, enraptured, glided along
        Without a sigh.
Our fingers touched, and our glances met,
Oh! those orbs of her soul I shall ne'er forget
For their soft, deep beauty haunteth me yet.

D

The depths of her dove-like eyes,
            Soft and bright,
Outpoured, like the sun o'er summer skies,
            A flood of light,
Which gleamed o'er a face surpassing fair,
For beauty, and love, and truth shone there,
And lightened her presence everywhere.

Her smile was as chaste and sweet
            As the silver sheen
Of the harvest moonlight when lovers meet,
And Evening's balmy zephyrs greet
            Their gentle queen.
Oh! when she smiled, there seemed to roll
O'er her brow an angel's aureole,
From the crystal deep of her radiant soul.

While every movement was blent
            With artless grace,
A something so pure and innocent,—
As if a diviner element
            Of holier race,
Mellowed each look with Affection's power,
Like sunny tints o'er a lovely flower,
When wooed by Noon in a vernal bower.

Soft as the nightingale's trill
   Was her voice,
And sweeping the chords of my soul at will,
Its love-winged tones with emotion's thrill,
   My heart rejoice ;
For Memory beams through the days gone by,
Dries up each tear-drop, hushes each sigh,
And brings back the moments when Phillis was nigh.

Oh ! fondly our bosoms glowed
   With new-born bliss,
When out from the springs of our being flowed
The love-rills which garrison Love's abode,
   And softly kiss
The blossoms of hope and virtue which bend
Entranced in their lustre, as onward they wend
To the sea of affection which hath no end.

Each look, every touch, was fraught
   With a magic spell,
Which deep in the woof of my bosom wrought,
Usurping the worship of every thought,
   And naught could quell :
And as Morning's dew-drops together run,
When warmed by the breath of the amorous sun,
Our heart-chords commingled in unison,

When the languishing passion-glow
          Of chaste desire
Entered our life-streams' quickened flow,
Transporting within us to and fro,
           Love's sacred fire!
Oh! sweet was the dream of that golden hour,
Golden the sway of its mystic power;
Golden the thought-links in Memory's dower

Which fetter my spirit once more
           In the aureate gleam
Of those cradled moments, now canopied o'er
With a halo as radiant as heretofore
           Of joy supreme:
Illuming my soul with Affection's light,
Upbearing my heart with Love's hallowed might,
And cheering the gloom of my passion's night.

For Fancy emblazons again
           The dawn of hope,
Which flashed like a phantom meteor-train
O'er the morn of affection, and burnished in vain
           Love's horoscope:
For the fond illusion evanished fast
As Duty's dark clouds o'er the orient passed,
And left the blue sky of my life o'ercast.

    *   *   *   *   *

The golden moments sped round,
              With rapture fraught,
And, mantled in ecstasy too profound,
We gave no heed to the warning-sound
              Of sober thought;
But ruthless Fate with his frown awoke
Our dreaming souls ere of love we spoke,
And the mystic spell of our reverie broke.

The fiat of Circumstance boomed!
              Ah, stern decree!
And our little golden hour was doomed
Henceforth to lie in the past entombed,
              No longer free
'Mid the halcyon languors of passion's noon,
As a sweet, inestimable boon
Which faded, alas! from our grasp too soon:

But hallowed in Memory's shrine,
              Its lustre beams
O'er Life's swift sand with a glow benign,
And in Solitude's calm with a sheen divine
              Engilds my dreams;
Like a golden gossamer woven through
That tangled skein, of chameleon hue,
Which the subtle fingers of Time undo.

Now the care-winged moments speed on
        'Mid smiles and tears;
The brief golden Hour which resplendently shone
With the hope-tinted gleam of affection has gone
        With the bygone years;
But, cherished in Memory's sacred embrace,
The future can never its beauty efface,
Nor sorrow make barren its dwelling-place.

NATHALIE.

'MID the bygone years—
  Stern with trial—dim with tears,
Golden sunshine, fragrance-laden, sometimes
    through the gloom appears:
But the last has bound my spirit with the scorpion-
    woof of Care,—
Bound my stricken, bleeding bosom, with the thews
    of wild despair;
Yet the image of thy martyred beauty lives un-
    fading there,
                Nathalie!
  One short year ago!
  How I wished each poignant throe
Would, in mercy, end the torture of my agonising
    woe;

As the weary months rolled o'er me, pining on the
    rack of Thought,—
All my cankered life-wounds gaping, every breath
    with anguish fraught,—
Broken-hearted, and my brain with frenzied hope-
    lessness distraught,
                Nathalie!
    When I saw thee last,
     As I stood unseen, aghast—
Stood behind a gloomy column, near the porch, as
    on you passed
From the holy fane's soft shadow, into Morning's
    rosy light,
To your titled bridegroom clinging, smileless, pale,
    nor bridal-bright,
Oh! that exodus in-ushered to my soul a blasting
    blight,
                Nathalie!
    Ah! the clash of bells,
    Blent with cheers in mighty swells,
Sounded to my fleeting senses like Despair's funereal
    knells;
As your stately carriage bounded o'er the road with
    roses strewn,—
As I pressed my burning brow upon the sculptured
    pillar-stone;
Oh, my passion, bartered idol! Godhead witnessed,—
    God alone!
                Nathalie!

But two years have gone,
  Since I stood at Silverlawn,
Stood beside you in the garden, as the purple
    summer dawn
Flushed the golden-barred horizon i' the east with
    morning's blush,
With your hand in mine, my darling, when from
    every brake and bush,
Echoed thro' the perfumed ether softest trills of
    lark and thrush,
                                Nathalie!

How your cheek grew pale,
  When I told "the old, old tale,"
Told in words that sighed and trembled like an
    aspen in the gale!
And I saw the vermeil heart-wave deepen o'er your
    pallid brow,
As within our panting souls Love hallowed each
    responsive vow;
Oh! the recollection rankles deeply in my bosom
    now,
                                Nathalie!

Purple-robed and fleet,
  Sped the morn with golden feet,
And dissolved the mists in fragrance round our
    blossom-wreathed retreat;
While we, unsuspicious, communed, — heedless,
    talked of hopes and fears,

Spoke with tongues beguiled by Love anent the
    joys of future years,
But, alas! our confidences fell within another's ears,
               Nathalie!
    Aye! a craven hind,—
    Basest of his pampered kind,—
Like a thirsting human vampire, unto all save
    lucre blind,—
Saw your white robe gently flutter, ere we gained
    the arbour's shade,
Sneaked anigh us thro' the laurels,—heard the
    solemn vows we made,
And, ere noon, our lives' fond secret to your father
    was betrayed,
               Nathalie!
    Proud and wealthy he,
    Proud of wealth and high degree,—
I could boast but honour, darling, and a mine
    of love for thee:
Love!—the love of a poor tutor, lowly-born and
    humbly-bred,
But as pure in every impulse as the blue sky over-
    head,
And as sacred as the halo of affection o'er the dead,
               Nathalie!
    Then, with curse and threat,—
    Ah! methinks I hear them yet,
And their angry, scathing fury, I can nevermore
    forget),—

Cursed, aye stricken, I was driven like a felon from
  his door,
Banished from my darling's presence,—banished
  ah ! for evermore!
Yet I answered nothing, dearest! God knows what
  I meekly bore, ·
                                    Nathalie!
    Two sad years ago,
  Two fond hearts, with love aglow,
Beat as one ; and every virtue heightened Hope's
  fair iris-bow;
But the curse of caste with blighting cruelty asunder
  rent
Those, whose souls, love-consecrate, in union Love
  had fondly blent,
And extinguished every star of hope in Love's fair
  firmament,
                                    Nathalie!
    Then a year of care;
  Mine,—a life of wild despair,
Thine,—Oh, Righteous Judge, in Heaven! Thou
  hast got the record there! ·
How my darling lived and suffered,—blighted by a
  father's pride ;
Broken-hearted, passive, martyred to become a
  dotard's bride,—
To become the old earl's wife! Ah, better thou
  had'st sooner died!
                                    Nathalie!

One short year,—o'ercast,
Swelled the record of the past;—
Ah, proud father, tears are useless, retribution
    cometh fast !
Pride claims yet another victim from thè base in-
    human mart,
Injured Love in mercy speeds the flight of Death's
    unerring dart,
And the sacrifice is made! Oh, God! Another
    broken heart !
                                    Nathalie!

Ah ! 'tis only gold,—
Source of wonders manifold !—
Gains admittance to the mart where human hearts
    are bought and sold !
Love and worth are only trifles in the Mammon-
    holden scale,
All the good, old-fashioned virtues, useless as " an
    old wife's tale ";—
But, oh fond love, thou hast gone where gold can
    nevermore assail ;
                                    Nathalie!

God ! Should this be so ?
Can the mocking, motley show
Passing, miming through the garish shrine of
    Fashion to and fro,
Constitute design's fulfilment in divinely-imaged
    man ?

Is the golden calf triumphant over all in Heaven's
    plan?
Tell me, spirit-love, whom Death set free from
    Fashion's cruel ban,
                        Nathalie !
    Truth lives not in vain !
    Though both rank and gold sustain
Flaunting Fashion's mighty Moloch in his diabolic
    reign !
No, thank Heaven ! And true manhood needs no
    meretricious art   [part !
To attest that it possesses man's divinest counter-
Earthly pomp may prate of wealth, but worth pro-
    claims a mind and heart,
                        Nathalie !
    Thus,—oh sweet, mine own !
    Mine, although thy soul hath flown
Upward to the seraph-hosts around the Father's
    mighty Throne.
Thus thy heart believed, and witnessed with a faith
    that scorned disguise,
Braved a father's ire, yet brooked enforced, unhal-
    lowed nuptial ties,
Nor would stifle love and conscience for the sake of
    social lies,
                        Nathalie !
    Cursèd be the might
    That would stifle truth and right,
And o'er honest manliness would dare to pour op-
    pression's blight !

To be poor is not unworthy,—to be humble matters
    not ;
Love may dwell within a castle, but securer in a cot,
And the pedigree of worth is that alone without a
    blot!
                        Nathalie!

    God ! Thy will be done !
    Love the victory hath won,
And I now await Thy summons to rejoin my sainted
    one !
Thou hast chastened, and I, longing, murmur not
    at Thy decree !
Oh, my darling ! I am longing from earth's war-
    fare to be free,
And find surcease of my sorrow,—rest and peace
    with God and thee,
                    Nathalie!

    Angel, pure and fair !
    Soon from earth's sad moil and care,
Love-delivered, I shall meet thee; love-rewarded,
    with thee share,
Lowlier, perhaps, but kindred ecstasies of love
    divine,
In Love's own infinitude, where peace shall ever-
    more be mine ;—
Therefore, wait I, oh, my darling, and shall never-
    more repine,
                   Nathalie!

BEAUTIFUL SUNSHINE.

Oh! the Sunshine, beautiful Sunshine,
Filling the earth with its glow benign,
Gilding the mountain-tops, gemming the sea
With a shimmering, golden galaxy.
Gleaming, beaming, soft and bright,
Beautiful Sunshine, heaven's light,
Kissing the brow of the Morning-queen,
Decking the sky with its radiant sheen,
Beautiful Sunshine, gladsome and wild,
Reflex of Love-light from Heaven beguiled.

Oh! the Sunshine, beautiful Sunshine,
Flash of the Day-god's mirthful eyne,
Cheering the dirge of the sighing breeze,
Waking to melody grim old trees;
Dancing, glancing over the brook,
Melting the dew with its roguish look,
Chasing the shadows over the hills,
Wooing the zephyrs, kissing the rills;
Beautiful Sunshine, gushing in love
From golden fountains in Heaven above.

Oh! bright Sunshine, beautiful Sunshine,
Joy of the poet's life is thine,
Darting thy gleams through his gloomy abode,
Like Angels of Hope from the presence of God.
Glowing, flowing o'er every street,
Climbing each steeple with nimble feet,—
Over the housetops, into each court,—
Painting old walls in thy gleeful sport,
Beautiful Sunshine, hushing the sigh
As it springs from the heart of the passer-by.

Glowing Sunshine, beautiful Sunshine,
Pouring thy rays o'er each hallowed shrine,
Laughing through grave-yards, over each tomb,
Driving the phantoms of Death and Gloom :
Straying, playing through every square,
Flirting with curls of each lady fair ;
Lingering over those coral lips,
Where Love his fragrant ambrosia sips ;
Beautiful Sunshine, wafting the breath
Of Angels over the vale of Death.

Golden Sunshine, beautiful Sunshine,
Winging the shades of the willow and pine,
Glinting thy rays o'er the Sovereign's crown,
Stealing through Infamy's dens up and down ;

Gliding, sliding through Flora's bowers,
Wiling the hearts of her choicest flowers;
Maddening Care with thy frolicsome freaks,
Tinting the blush on the maiden's cheeks,
Pouring thy radiance o'er Life's dark way,
And cheering sad hearts with thy glowing ray.

Beautiful Sunbeams, children of Sunshine,
Benisons breathed by a Father Divine,
Robing the tears which have strayed from their fold,
Like diamonds shrined in a halo of gold;
Peeping, creeping through eyries of crime,
Pencilling over the ruins of Time,
Mantling over the rose-bloom of health,
Shaming the flare on the tinsel of wealth;
Beautiful sunbeams, bewitching the hours,
And gladdening ever this fair world of ours.

    *   *   *   *   *

What do the beautiful sunbeams teach ?
What are the sermons the sunbeams preach,
Shining alike over good and ill ?
Peace upon earth,—content, good-will;
Virtuous love in the breasts of men,
Unity fostered by brethren !
Balm for the wounded, succour for need,
Charity, courting nor class nor creed,

Truth in the bosoms of all and each,
Such is a sermon the Sunbeams preach!

Dry the sad tears from the penitent's cheek,
Strengthen the hearts of the timid and weak,
Let the soft flood of a merciful soul
Over the faults of humanity roll;
Chide not in harshness, anger, or pride,
But waft the appeal of affection, to glide
Like a pitying ray of the generous sun,
Through the overcast soul of the erring one;
And beckon the child of Misfortune with smiles
From Infamy's grasp—Immorality's wiles.

Let freedom and honesty, concord and worth,
With kindness and sympathy, flourish on earth;
Let the strong help the weak, and the weak trust
    the strong,
Let both do the right, while they censure the wrong,
And, as patriot-saints, guard our Isles of the West,
With swords ever ready to help the oppressed.
May Virtue's and Liberty's flags be unfurled,
While Britain's Evangel proclaims to the world
That the Father of Mercies is waiting to roll
His Heavenly Sunshine o'er every soul!

CHACUN À SON GOÛT.

THE Lady Bertha walks to-day
Around her castle's walls,
And sparkling dew-drops vie to kiss
Each footstep as it falls;
Amid the flowers, no flower more sweet
Smiles on the sunny slope,
Her every movement, in its grace,
Rivals the antelope.
They say her heart is pure and good,
Although the pride of earth
Hangs on her soft, majestic brow
Like clouds of summer birth.

The virgin innocence of Love
Gleams through her light-blue eyes;
In golden waves her braidless hair—
Like aureate Morning's rise—
Flows with an undulating sheen,
Wooing the perfumed breeze,
While song-birds warble forth her praise
In sweetest symphonies.

Well may Sir Hubert, her betrothed,
Walk proudly by her side,
And long to clasp her to his breast—
His own—his darling bride!

*   *   *   *   *

Our village maidens work to-day,—
Toil in the golden fields,
And with them brown-eyed Jenny May
Her glancing sickle wields.
With merry laugh, and lightsome heart,
Where lurks nor guile nor care,
She sheds her cheerfulness around,
And gladdens everywhere.
Her dimpled chin and rosy cheeks
The artist well might prize,
But Art is powerless to depict
The heaven of her eyes.

Affection's gleam, immaculate,
Smiles on her lovely face,
And health's soft rose-tint on her brow
Heightens her loveliness.
No sweeter wildflower, fresh and fair,
Blooms in the fields to-day;
Nor purer maiden breathes on earth
Than brown-eyed Jenny May!

I'd rather win Love's sweet reward
From her,—our village pride,—
Than Lady Bertha's jewelled hand,
And all her wealth beside!

WILDFLOWERS.

THRO' the meadows, down the lanes,
On the hill-sides, in the dells,—
Wooed by sunbeams on the plains,
Wooed by shadows in the fells;
By the streamlet and the lake,
Ever modest, fresh, and fair,—
By the hedge-row, and the brake,—
Wildflowers blossom everywhere!

Richer gems in Nature's crown
Win from men the higher praise,
Yet they merit not renown
More than those, whose softer rays
Blend their mellow, tinted light
With the flash, tho' bright as noon,
As, upon the brow of Night
Stars shed lustre round the moon.

Dearer, sweeter far to me
Are the simple, common flowers
Blooming by the road-side, free
As sunshine, or the fleeting hours,
Than the costly blossoms prized,
Propped, and pruned by haughty Art;—
Better worth, tho' oft despised,
Than beauty, oft without a heart!

Smiling in the fragrant hedge,
Nodding to the crystal brook,
Nestled in the waving sedge,
Bosomed in the shady nook;
Chaste as sunbeams: pure and sweet
As the soul-fraught kiss of love,—
Weaving joys around our feet,
While they point our hearts above!

Creeping, peeping here and there,
Climbing round the giant trees,
Perfuming the summer air,
Sporting with the summer breeze:—
O'er the mountains, thro' the woods,
Gemming Nature's verdant sod,
Shrined within her solitudes,
Alone with Nature and her God!

Oh ! ye Wildflowers, fresh and gay,
Simple blossoms tho' ye be,
Blooming o'er Life's common way,
Ye are dearest far to me.
Meek, yet lovely, pure and sweet
As the zephyr's fragrant sigh,
Tho' ye blossom at my feet
I shall not unmoved pass by!

Blessings oft in simple guise
Are bestrewn around us all,
Yet, too selfish and unwise,
We neglect them as they fall
O'er Life's purpose-hallowed road,
From the genial skies above,
From the infinite abode
Of mercy, tenderness, and love.

So the Wildflowers,—scarcely prized,
Blooming freely everywhere,—
Like small blessings are despised,
Tho' the seal of God they wear :
But, when men themselves are laid
In the cold and silent tomb,
Nourished by its mournful shade,
Simple native flowers will bloom !

Oh! in Nature's varied store
There is nothing undesigned;
Every pebble on Life's shore
Bears its lesson to mankind:
And each tiny way-side flower
Has its mission from on high,—
Teaches men with mighty power
How to live, and how to die!

———————

CHARLES DICKENS,

BORN, FEBRUARY 7TH, 1812. DIED, JUNE 9TH,
1870.

THE people weep in vain,
Their darling son is dead!
The noble heart is still,—
The gentle soul has fled.
No more the toiling hand
Will wield the magic pen
Which pleaded for the Right,
And swayed the hearts of men.

No more the genial smile
Will gleam upon that face,
Which, shrined in every heart,
Hallowed its dwelling-place.
No more those soul-lit eyes
Shall flash their humour now;
No more the blaze of wit
Shall gild that lofty brow.

The mighty master-mind
Which wove Truth's holy spell,
Which cheered our hearths and homes,
And tolled Oppression's knell,
Now sleeps—in Death's embrace,
'Mid silence of the tomb,
Leaving Mankind to mourn
In universal gloom.

Hushed be all party strife,
Forgotten selfish grief,
To-day the nations mourn
The conquest of a chief
Who lived within their hearts,
And scorned or rank or place;
Who toiled and fought alone
To benefit his race.

The fell Destroyer's breath
On cruel wings has sped,
And smitten England's pride—
The people's friend is dead !
Oh ! Earth is sad to-day,
And Genius weeps in vain,—
When shall the womb of Time
Produce his like again ?

His was the power, but his,
To rule all hearts at will,
To spread convulsive mirth—
To waft emotion's thrill ;
His was the fertile brain
Which bound the souls of earth,
Where eager nations stood
To hail each creature's birth.

Hypocrisy and Cant
Paled at his very name,
And shrunk their coward heads
Beneath that powerful flame
Which scorched foul Error's wings,
And poured its flood of light
O'er Prejudice's gloom
And Superstition's night.

The pioneer of Truth,—
The champion of Right,—
The Shakespeare of our age
Has vanished from our sight;
But neither Time nor Death,
With all their mystic arts,
His loved, immortal name
Can steal from English hearts.

No ! while the wheels of Time
O'er Earth's dominions roll,
Shall DICKENS' simple name
Illumine Fame's fair scroll ;
And each succeeding race
Will praise the giant mind
Which led the hearts of men,—
A blessing to mankind.

OLD LETTERS.

WITHIN a nook behind the tapestry
Which hangs around my chamber's time-stained
    walls,—
A spot where sunshine's coruscating ray,
Or moonlight's silvery pencil seldom falls,—

I found the packet which I gaze on now,
And which I placed there many years ago,
When Love conspired so cruelly with Death
To cause my cherished idol's overthrow.

Tho' Time has stamped his signet on my brow,
And threads of grey proclaim life's autumn eve,
Yet blissful thoughts of happy, halcyon hours
Around youth's portrait verdant chaplets weave.
Fond memory loves to paint the golden dream,
Which passed so sweetly o'er my spell-bound soul,
And living, love-fraught visions of the past
O'er my lone heart a flood of blessing roll.

Ah me! my rankling life-wound bleeds afresh,
Which Time, (the skilled physician who sustains
The broken spirit bound to earth's rude wheels),
Had well-nigh banished; but my anguish wanes
At sight of you, my youth's fond bosom friends;
Now ye are brown and sere, but living still,
Like her whom once you crowned with true love's joy,
Whose stricken soul e'en now your voices thrill.

Sweet messengers, who once in years gone by,
With hope illumed the Summer of my heart,—
Who now again, when life is waxing old,
Your sacred radiance o'er the past impart,—

Your mouldering pages, stained with many a tear,
Speak comfort in a hallowed tone to me,
And every line, by fond affection traced,
Is graved within the shrine of memory.

Methinks I live again in Love's fair sphere;
The gorgeous scenes with golden visions teem,
And elfin music borne on zephyrs' wings
Steals o'er my senses like a holy dream.
My soul's enchanter guides my timid steps,
And shows fresh beauties to my wond'ring gaze,
While countless choristers, with melting strain,
A grateful anthem to their monarch raise.

Ah! cruel Death-king, by whose withering breath,
Were melted those sweet day-dreams of my youth,—
By one fell stroke of whose unsparing hand
My happy heart was rent in twain, forsooth;—
Why did you leave me thus in grief to pine,
Affection-martyred through this vale of tears,
Why take the sun which lit my passion's noon,
And spare me drear and lone so many years?

Ah! dear old letters, Faith's ambassadors,
My erring spirit gently you reprove,
And aid my drooping, chastened soul to bear
Her galling burden to Love's courts above.

There shall I meet my sainted love again,
Where neither fate nor death can part us more;
There shall I tread the golden streets with him
" Who is not dead,—who is but gone before."

In youth's bright morn ye gave new life to me,
Ere doomed to bear Love's cruel sacrifice,
And now, when Life's sad twilight draweth near,
Thy voice directs my thoughts to Paradise ;—
No more, forgotten, shall ye sleep in gloom,
But near me always shall your presence be,
And, fondly cherished in my inmost heart,
I'll shrine thy precepts in my memory.

MYRA.

I saw her when a timid, blushing maid,
When youth, and hope, and joy illumed her brow;
I saw her in the April of her life,
Ere Love had sought to steal her vestal vow.
Ere long affection wrought its potent spell
Upon my dreaming, solitary soul ;
And imperceptibly, by mystic art,
Entrammelled me, as glides the silent ghoul

Through moss-clad ruin, crumbling fast away,
And fraught with history. Her presence then
Shone forth within me with a shimmering gleam,
Which filled my heart (as through each glade and
    glen
The sunshine gleams, illuming vale and hill),
And stirred my bosom with Hope's sacred thrill.
A little while, and Beauty's lavish hand
Had decked her in the Junehood of her prime;
'Twas then the vernal, love-tinct passion-flower
Burst into Love's ethereal summer-time.
We revelled in the balmy, fragrant air,
We gloated o'er fresh beauties day by day,
We basked beneath our sun's effulgent sheen,
And wist not that such scenes could pass away.
Soft zephyrs kissed my Myra's glowing cheek,
And sunbeams wooed the heaven of her smile;
And song-birds, carolling their sweetest strains,
Would cease their flight to gaze on her awhile;
Then tender vows in fondest accents given,
Were heard and registered by Love in Heaven.
Now mellow Autumn sheds her ruddy light,
And o'er fair Nature wafts her sickly breath;
While deepening shades, and sombre russet
    hues
Suffused around—foretell the dawn of death.

A dewy rose-bud, kissed by noon-day beam—
Bursts into life, a lovely, perfect flower;
Then rudely grasped, it droops its smiling head,
And fades and perishes within an hour:—
So was my Myra; as an op'ning rose,
When Love had poured the radiance of his sun
Upon her soul, and waked new life within;
Then Autumn breathed my darling's cheek upon,
And hectic flush on pallid brow revealed
The subtle death-germ in her breast concealed.
Unpitying Winter spares nor flower nor fruit,
But, ruthless still,—the analogue of death,—
Spreads desolation o'er each lovely scene;
Yet, (e'en as cares oft try our simple faith),
He devastates, that earth may smile anon
More sweetly far. As infant sunbeams lie
Enshrined within a mass of gloomy clouds,—
(Like Virtue garrisoned by Poverty !)—
So Summer sleeps in Winter's cold embrace,
To wake again with increased loveliness.
Thus did the summer of my soul depart,
When Myra, hast'ning to the arms of death,
Prayed long for him to whom her heart was
        given,
Then smiled, and gently fell asleep in Heaven !
Transplanted from the garden of our earth,—

Where cold, harsh winds oft blast the tender bud ;—
(Alas ! too often Life's rude cares assail
The virgin flower of Beauty's womanhood !)
Now Myra blooms where fragrant zephyrs woo
Celestial sunbeams in the bowers of Love,
Where Peace, and Life, and Light perennially
Flourish in Heaven's Elysian courts above.
Her happy spirit, ever hovering near,
Speaks to my heart in fondest, sweetest strain;
And, Hope directing me in whispers soft,
Will cheer me till in Heaven we meet again.
Spirit of Life and Love ! increase my faith
And guide my spirit through the Vale of Death!

THE PASTOR'S DEATH.

(FOUNDED ON FACT.)

AGAIN a hallowed Sabbath morn
Is ushered into birth,
And Nature with a holier voice
Her anthem swells o'er earth ;
Again the solemn-sounding bells
Our drooping spirits move,
While unseen angels whisper peace,
And tell of Heaven's love.

But wherefore are the people sad,
And bowed in tongueless grief,—
Why are their hearts with sorrow fraught,
While tears bring no relief?
Ah! ruthless Death, thy stern decree,
Which spares nor good nor great,
Hath called a loved one from their midst,
And left them desolate.

The loved apostle of his God,
With simple, child-like faith,—
Victorious over Satan's wiles,
Triumphant over death,—
Has heard a voice from Heaven call,
" Faithful! thy race is run!"
And joyful angels cry aloud,
" Servant of God! Well done!"

And on that peaceful holy morn,—
When in the house of prayer
His loving flock with joy await,
To worship with him there,—
His soul descends the vale of death,
And mounts on seraphs' wings,
To sing the Song of the Redeemed
Before the King of Kings!

F

A noble brother of his race,
Who toiled from youth to age
To benefit his fellow-men,
And smooth life's pilgrimage,—
A gallant soldier in the van,
Where Truth and Mercy strove
To consecrate the sons of men,
And lead their hearts above:—

The faithful friend of fallen man,—
A soul of precious worth,—
A heart which overflowed with love,
Has passed away from earth;
But, oh! unnumbered hearts still hear
That gentle, pleading voice,
Which led them over Jordan's stream,
And made their souls rejoice.

The benefactor of the poor,
Whose cares he made his own,
It needs no sculptured monument
To tell of him who's gone!
For, ever like a summer cloud,
Shall hover o'er his head,
The hearts he cheered,—the minds he taught,—
The souls he comforted.

The hallowed work he wrought below,
The name he leaves behind,
The pure example of his life,
From sire to son consigned,
Will shimmer like a sunbeam through
The corridors of Time,
And tell of him who lived to make
The life of man sublime.

The dear, familiar face we loved
Will smile on us no more,
Yet angels whisper to each heart,—
" Not lost—but gone before"!
The kindly heart,—the mighty tongue,—
Lie silent in the tomb,
But, in the garden of his God
That soul shall ever bloom.

Then, wherefore weep ?   The loss we mourn
Is his immortal gain ;
The noble works he wrought on earth
For ever shall remain,
To speak of him whose gifted mind
Was filled with Heaven's love,—
The sinner's friend,—the humble saint
Whom God hath called above.

SONG.

Love's sweet lyre, unheeded, slumbers
Sadly in this heart of mine,
Lady, wake its softest numbers
With that magic power of thine.
Sweep its chords with love-taught fingers,
Long unstrung and mute they've lain ;
Strike, where fond Affection lingers
To applaud each hallowed strain.

Take my heart ! and Love will gladly
Tune each string with sacred fire,
Lady, pine not thus so sadly,
Take my heart, and strike the lyre !
Thy sweet smile alone can waken
From its sleep each thrilling tone,
Lady, leave it not forsaken,
Seize it, use it as thine own !

IMPROMPTU.

I choose a proverb for my theme,
And pray you to its truth attend,
However hopeless things may seem,
"It never is too late to mend " !

To err is human ; and the best
From Right's straight path may sometimes wend,
But yet hope's cheerful words attest
" It never is too late to mend " !

And tho' again, and yet again
You may have raised a fallen friend,
Still faithful to your trust remain,—
" It never is too late to mend " !

Then, if a weaker brother err,
Let kindness with your counsel blend,
And of success do not despair,—
" It never is too late to mend " !

ADA ;

A DAY-DREAM.

WEAK and weary, toiling upward,
Onward o'er Life's rugged way,
Sick at heart, and faltering,—fainting
In the noon of manhood's day,—
Down I sank upon the roadside,
Near the borders of a stream,
Writhing, until Fancy, passing,
Bound me in a golden dream.

As I slept, methought a spirit—
Blushing like a new-made bride,
Lovely as the smile of morning—
Glided gently to my side;
Softly, coyly, she caressed me,
And her presence seemed to thrill,
With a power rejuvenescent,
Through my spell-bound soul at will.

Then she spoke in accents tender,—
Sweeter than the song of dove,—
And I saw, as she bent o'er me,
On her brow was written "Love !"
" Rise, poor mortal, weak and lonely,
" Come ! let me thy cares assuage ;   .
" And accept a guide to cheer thee
" On thy dreary pilgrimage !"

Then, methought, I was transported
Through Elysian, halcyon bowers,—
Through the music-laden ether,—
Through the breath of sweetest flowers,
To the dwelling of the Spirit
On whose brow was written "Love,"—
Whose enrapturing voice was gentler,
Sweeter than the song of dove.

Then she pointed to a picture
'Circled with a rosy wreath,
And the simple name of " Ada "
Glittered strangely underneath.
Long I gazed, enchanted,—spell-bound,—
At the portrait of a maid
Whose surpassing beauty bound me;
Till the Spirit fondly said,—

" Look, poor mortal, on the image
" Of the guide I promised thee;
" Seek her on thy journey thither,
" Where she waits thee joyfully:
" Love and trust her—she is worthy;
" And remember, if you fall,—
" If you sink beneath your burden,
" I shall hasten at your call!"

Then her sister, Hope, espied me,
And, with radiant face drew near
To the spot where I was standing,
Whispering sweetly in mine ear:—
" Mortal, seek our darling hand-maid,
" Whom my sister has bestowed,
" To conduct your fearful footsteps
" O'er life's rugged, gloomy road.

" She is lovely as the morning,
" Gentle, amiable, good;
" And the spirit of affection
" Sanctifies her maidenhood.
" Oh, thou solitary mortal,
" Seek her as you upward press,
" And the lamp of Faith will guide you
" Safely through the wilderness.

" My existence is eternal !
" I shall ever hover near
" To reanimate thy bosom
" If thy soul is dark or drear;
" Shun Despair's unhallowed portal,
" Or I must abandon thee;
" Ever toil, with noble effort,
" And, when weary, summon me!"

Thus she said, and, disappearing,
Pointed to the picture there,—
To the portraiture of Ada,
Sweetly, exquisitely fair.
Presently, like lingering shadows
Melted by Aurora's light,
Vanished the celestial vision
Softly from my wondering sight.

Then the spell which so enchained me,
Evanescing like my dream,
I awoke upon Life's roadside,
Near the borders of a stream.
Now refreshed, and hopeful, joyful
I pursue my onward way,—
Seeking for the lovely Ada,
In the noon of manhood's day!
Fondly, dearly, I shall love her,
For she's gentle, cheerful, good,
And the spirit of affection
Sanctifies her maidenhood!

TWO STARS.

THE glory-roll of England bears a name
Which Love and Genius will for ever guard
Within the portals of immortal Fame!—
The glorious name of Avon's peerless bard!—
Of one, but one, if not inspired, yet far
Exalted in the altitude of mind
Above his fellows, like a full-orbed star
Amid the lesser hosts : who judged mankind

And human-nature as a demi-god,—
Sounded their depths and shallows, and portrayed
With master-hand their faults and foibles; awed
A wond'ring world by mirroring each shade
Of life and character,—and deftly limned
Men's passions, virtues, vices, hopes, and fears;
SHAKESPEARE! Whose genius shall remain un-
    dimmed,
While English hearts throb on thro' future years!

*	*	*	*	*	*

Of smaller magnitude, yet softly bright,
And chaste as Hesperus, serenely gleams
Another orb, which sheds its hallowed light—
(Like Hope's fair iris-tints thro' lovers' dreams)—
Over the spacious round, where Fame records
The worth of Britons. Oh! how sweet the name
Of him, who, spurning tinselly rewards,
And empty titles, stamped the brand of shame
On foul Injustice,—trampled on the head
Of base Hypocrisy, and boldly strove
To tear the mask from Ignorance: who sped
The streams of kindness, charity, and love
Thro' homes and hearts innumerable; sought
The people's welfare, and his country's good,—

To aid the poor and weak; and ever wrought
To bind all men in love and brotherhood;—
Who shed a halo round our hopes and fears,
And taught us to be heroes in earth's strife,—
The gentle master of our smiles and tears,—
DICKENS, the Shakespeare of familiar life!

SISTER, I'M COMING HOME!

ON RECEIVING SOME BEAUTIFUL LINES FROM MY
SISTER, ENTITLED, "BROTHER, COME HOME!"

SISTER, thy loving message, o'er the deep
In Love's soft whisper to my heart hath come;
My gladdened soul within her cage doth leap,
And now, my darling, I am coming home!
        Sister, I'm coming home!

The Winter heralds had announced their king
When last I gazed upon our loved fire-side;
He fled! then passed the vernal round of Spring,
And now, in Summer's golden morning-tide,
        Sister, I'm coming home!

I've toiled in hope and love beyond the sea,
Yet Memory ever hallowed each fair scene
In that sweet spot which is so dear to me,
While Hope still cheered me with her glow serene,
    And now, I'm coming home !

If dark, umbrageous clouds have crossed my
    path,
Bright, sunny thoughts of home have cheered my
    breast;
The darkest cloud a silver lining hath,—
The weariest spirit will at length have rest,—
    And now, I'm coming home !

Home to the sunshine of a mother's love,—
Home to receive a father's fond caress,—
Home where fair sisters, and kind brothers prove
That Life is no unhallowed wilderness,—
    Sister, I'm coming home !

Methinks I feel the love-bound, mute embrace,
And see Love's tears suffuse each soul-lit eye ;
Methinks I see each sweet familiar face,
And hear the bliss-inspiring melody—
    " Oh ! Welcome ! Welcome home !"

Oh ! how the deep emotions of my soul,
Thrill my glad bosom like a holy spell,
Oh ! how I count the days as on they roll,
And oh ! the joy I feel no tongue can tell,
    Because I'm coming home !

Sister, thy loving message o'er the deep,
In Love's soft whisper to my heart hath come,
My gladdened soul within her cage doth leap,
And now, my darling, I am coming home,
    Sister, I'm coming home !

MY CHILDHOOD'S HOME.

However our lives in the past have been saddened,—
However our hearts have been scarred in the strife,—
Fond Memory gleams thro' the Eden of childhood,
And gilds with her sunshine the noon-day of life.
How sweet, then, to think of those days gone for
    ever,
When youth's balmy morning our young hearts
    o'erjoyed ;—

When green fields of home, and the streamlet, and
     wildwood,
Afforded us pleasure, with care unalloyed.
    Home of my childhood! Eden of loveliness!
    Hallowed with father's love, and mother's.
     tenderness;
    Shared with a brother's smile, and sister's fond
     caress,
           My childhood's home!
      Fondly memory lingers o'er thee,
      Tho' now far from thee I roam;
      Sunshine in life's dreary desert,
      Home of my heart, my childhood's home!

Methinks now I hear the soft voice of the stream-
     let,—
I see the old abbey with ivy-clad towers,
And smile on the forms of my school-fellows round
     me,—
How blissful the thought of those halcyon hours!
Once more, my young bosom with happiness
     glowing,
I cull scented flowers from the dear mossy lane,
Where blackberries grew, and the nectary haw-
     thorn,—
Oh! fondly I gaze on that picture again!

Home of my childhood, oh, how I love thee !
Pure is that love, as the blue sky above thee,
'Shrined in my heart, there is nought can
remove thee,
  My childhood's home !
 Fondly memory lingers o'er thee,
 Tho' now far from thee I roam ;
 Sunshine in life's dreary desert,—
 Home of my heart, my childhood's home.

Bright as the stars in the blue vault of heaven
Is Memory's vision of youth's golden dream ;
And the fair scenes of childhood, engirt by affection,
Illumine my soul with immaculate gleam.
Tho' now care-oppressed in the land of the stranger,
Tho' sundered we be by the fathomless deep,
My last wish will be, when my warfare is ended
On thy tender bosom to sleep my last sleep. [den,
 Home of my childhood ! Life's cares may mad-
 Pining for thee, my lone spirit may sadden,
 Yet Memory ever my fond heart will gladden,
  My childhood's home!
 Fondly memory lingers o'er thee,
 Tho' now far from thee I roam ;
 Sunshine in life's dreary desert,—
 Home of my heart,—my childhood's home !

ST. VALENTINE'S DAY.

HAIL, fair Erato ! I pray thee
Aid this puling muse of mine,
To accord a hearty welcome
To our good Saint Valentine !

Dear old friend, with joy we greet thee,
Welcome thou to each fond heart,—
Gentle, cherished necromancer
Of Love's hallowed, mystic art !

Once again the morning dawneth,
Bright with love, and mirth, and joy,
When each heart awaits a message
From dear Cupid,—blessed boy !

See each face with pleasure beaming,
See those eyes with fond hope shine !
Blest and happy is the morning
Of our dear old Valentine!

Expectation fills each bosom,
Every heart with rapture glows,
And Love's blush, o'er Beauty's dimples,
Bloometh like a virgin-rose.

Hark ! the postman's welcome footstep,
Doubly sweet his loud rat-tat,
As he hurries on o'erburdened,—
Ladies, dear, *you* know with *what !*

Every window teems with beauty,—
Willing slaves of Love's fair shrine,—
And each heart beats faster,—louder,—
Anxious for its Valentine.

Even Frizzle in the kitchen,—
Love-sick maiden,—restless seems,
And awaits with weary longing
Something from her precious " Jeames "!

Hear those joyous exclamations,—
" I know who it's from !" " So nice !"
" O, you naughty girl, I told you,
" You had vanquished Alderdice ! "

Ah ! that look of disappointment !
See the postman pass yon door ;
See poor Amy with vexation
Tap her foot upon the floor !

In the brightest golden noon-day,
Gloom oft through the radiance peers,
So the happy heart's soft sunshine
Sweetest smiles through Beauty's tears.

G

Happiness presides supremely
On this morn of Valentine,
Tho' some truants fail to forward
Love's old message, " Ever thine !"

Many a heart has been elated,
Which was erst disposed to pine,
By that little perfumed *sachet*,
Saying " Dearest, be thou mine !"

Loving hearts are oft united,—
Souls in unison combine,—
Through the sweet, seductive pleading
Of some tender Valentine.

May fond Love and Truth, engrafted
In each heart, with Faith entwine,—
May each happy pair still welcome
Each return of Valentine !

Dear old friend, with joy we greet thee,
Welcome thou to every heart,
Gentle, cherished necromancer
Of Love's hallowed, mystic art !

WHITHER?

I'VE sat beside a laughing, gurgling stream,
And seen young sunbeams wanton on its breast;
I've seen the water-lily's pouting lips
By the soft ripples of the stream caressed;—
I've seen a leaf, into the crystal flood
Borne from the bosom of its parent tree,—
I've seen the river dashing madly through
Its rocky channel,—bounding to the Sea—

Onward!

I've seen the morning sun-glow melt the clouds
Which, cradled, lay upon the mountain-tops,
And watched the sunbeams kiss away the dew
Which crowned the op'ing flowers with pearly drops:
I've seen the sea-gulls in their lofty flight,
And culled the beauties of the glittering shore,—
I've heard the sky-lark swell her hymn of praise,
And seen her through the azure welkin soar—

Upward!

I've stood with saddened heart, and tearful eye
Beside the death-bed of a lovely child;
I've heard him whisper softly as he slept,
And felt that angels beckoned as he smiled;

I've lingered when the silver cord was loosed,—
When Life's last flickering, vital spark had gone,
And knew full well a young,immortal soul—
Borne on Love's wings by cherubim—had flown
                                        Heavenward !

I see Life's billowy deep on every side,
And hear its awful chorus of unrest ;
I see a mighty argosy of souls
Sportively tossed upon its heaving breast,
As, in a storm, the struggling ship is borne
High on the surging billow-crest ; then drawn
Into the seething, fathomless, abyss,
While the impetuous ocean bears her on—
                                        Whitherward ?

There is a land of beauty, rest, and peace,
Beyond the limits of life's angry sea,
Where Love Divine with gentle sway presides
Amid the bowers of immortality !
Oh ! struggling mortal ! hear Faith's " still small
    voice,"
As she directs thee o'er the treacherous main,—
Hear Love's sweet whisper in the ocean's roar,—
Hear Mercy call thee in the hurricane—
                                        Thitherward !

                    ————————

THE PURSUIT OF PLEASURE.

(Suggested by Sir Noel Paton's Picture.)

" THE streamlet hastens from its crystal source,
To swell the bosom of the mighty river,
Both towards the ocean speed their onward course,
And hasting fleetly on,—go on for ever!
To-day is stricken, yesterday is dead,
To-day is dying, yesterday is buried !
To-day the bride is to the altar led,—
A widow to the grave will soon be carried !

" Men were created to experience Life
In all the fulness of its varied pleasures,—
To cull its roses, and avoid its strife,
And hoodwink Father Time with lively measures !
Bid care begone, and pass the flowing bowl,
While careless mirth confuses thoughts of duty !
The charms of Beauty guide our ' flow of soul,'—
Our 'feast of reason' boasts Mirth, Wine, and Beauty!

"Give Time no thought, nor heed what others teach
Anent the power and purpose of existence ;
Let them rave on, and practice what they preach,
To live and die requires not their assistance !

The Past is gone ! the Present is our own !
The Future may be fraught with joy or sorrow,
But, while our pathway is with roses strewn,
We'll laugh to-day, and think of grief to-morrow ! "

So sings the worldling, while the wheels of Time
Are o'er the earth with silent speed revolving ;
So, too, the libertine, while luring Crime
Despair's mad fire is in his cup dissolving !
And thus they wing the garish hours away,
Amid the vapid joys in which they revel :—
Damn every moment of their little day,—
Deny the Godhead, and defy the devil !

But yet not all is Life to them a dream
Of golden noons, blue skies, and rosy bowers,—
Of joys perennial flushing through the gleam
Of cloudless sunshine, redolent with flowers !
Within their breasts Remorse's direful gloom
Blights life and hope, whilst outraged Conscience
      lashes,
And goads their spirits in a living tomb,
Wherein the sweets of being turn to ashes !

The syren whom they worship,—for whose smile
They damn their souls and prostitute their reason,—

Though but a myth who seemeth to beguile
The solemn hours of Life's decisive season,—
Allures with wanton acts, and deftly weaves
Her scorpion-web insensibly around them,
Then tears her mask off, as her dupes she leaves,
To learn too late it was Despair who bound them

Just as the moth, whose too ambitious wings
Court the bright flame that will at length destroy
    them,
So foolish men, when lustful Pleasure sings,—
Charmed with the voice,—the smile which will
    decoy them
From wisdom, virtue, reason, truth, and worth,—
Peril their souls to win her false caresses,
And from Life's power and purpose wander forth
To learn how cruelly her yoke oppresses :—

To find remorse where they expected bliss,—
Instead of happiness, despair and malice,—
To feel a serpent's tooth in every kiss,
And quaff perdition from her fragrant chalice !
Yet they pursue her still bewitching form,
And, though she curse will smile and follow after,
As the poor clown who feeds care's canker-worm,
Paling with anguish, earns his bread by laughter !

Oh, soon, how soon ! the void unreal joys
Of lawless passion vanquish their pursuer ;
Oh, soon unhallowed Pleasure's sway destroys
The godlike element in those who woo her !
Ah, soon, — too late, alas ! — with Conscience
    seared,
And souls defiled, from Folly's dream they
    waken,
To find themselves shunned, stricken, wretched,
    feared,—
By hope, health, fame and friends alike forsaken !

Their future ? Ah, still, Pity's soul-sped tears
Are flowing freely ; Mercy still is pleading ;
And angel-hosts, amid celestial spheres,
Before the Great White Throne are interceding !
Look up, ye bounden mammon-martyrs ! See
" Our Father's " arms outstretched in love from
    Heaven !
His mighty hands alone can set ye free !
Look up ! Repent, believe, and be forgiven !

To err is human ; yet 'tis well to guide
The footsteps of a weak and erring brother ;
To counsel kindly,—with affection chide,
And do to him as we would have another

Do unto us. And, though he, stumbling, falls
Again and yet again, be ours to cherish,—
With patient hearts, and Hope which naught appals,
This *duty :* raise him ; leave him not to perish !

HEROISM.

THOSE who amid the cares of life
Its power and purpose fitly scan,
And in the hottest of the strife
Will stoop to aid their fellow-man ;—
Who toil and trust through weal and woe,
Nor seek for self the highest good,
But treat with justice friend and foe,
And strive to join in brotherhood,—
With chains of love, all ranks of men,
Whate'er their talents or estate,—
Maintain the truth, and rightly ken
The *good* alone as truly *great !*—
Yet o'er the failings of the weak
The cloak of mercy gently spread,—
Listen whene'er the fallen speak,
And penitential tears are shed.

Those who are earnest when they chide,
In counsel kind, in patience strong,—
Who cheer with hope, nor basely hide
The charms of right when blaming wrong.
Whose loving hearts rejoice to win,
By kindly words and noble deeds,—
The fallen from the depths of sin,—
The weak from vice when want misleads ;—
Who in the path of duty plod
To Providence's will resigned,
And live to glorify their God,—
To love and benefit their kind.
Such are the nobles of the earth,
Whose pure nobility outshines
From Virtue's pedigree of worth ;—
Great heroes and true heroines !

IN THE TOILS.

ERSTWHILE, a pensive, melancholy youth,
I've plodded on from day to day alone,
An earnest student in Dame Nature's school,—
Loving her every look, and touch, and tone.

But now my mind is restless as the bee
Which sips the sweets of every fragrant flower;
My cherished day-dreams one by one have fled,—
My charming books have lost their magic power!

Philosophy compels me to believe
That Nature governs by unerring laws,
And, though a tyro, I have learned to know
That each *effect* must have a parent *cause !*
Why then this change? My quondam hopes and joys
Now fail to cheer, as they were wont to do;
The spirit of Unrest broods o'er my soul,
And Ennui chains my mind in chaos too.

       *   *   *   *   *

There's a fair, sweet maid just over the way,
And Love caught me looking across one day,
And aimed at us both, as he flew away!

She's as gay and bright as a restless rill
Whose musical murmur is never still,
And she sweeps o'er the chords of my heart at will!

From her eyes of fairest, mildest blue
There gleams a soul of the purest sheen;
And her smile, like the rose's crown of dew,
Hath woven its spell round my heart, I ween.

Oh, those eyes of bluest brightness!
Oh, that brow of softest whiteness!
And that step of graceful lightness—
           They enchant me!

While a flow of golden tresses,—
Which the love-sick breeze caresses,—
And a look no tongue expresses,—
           Ever haunt me!

Oh, you teasing, wayward fairy!—
Ever of your sunshine wary,—
How your fitful fancies vary,
           I know best!

But while, with a will unbroken,
You reject Love's golden token,—
While one word remains unspoken,
           I can't rest!

Oh, my darling, do have pity!
Every thought is ever thine.:
I am weary,—Life is dreary
Till you promise to be mine!

LINES.

EUTERPE, come! assist my muse
From out thy gifted throng to choose
                    The best!
Say who most sweetly swept thy lyre,—
Who most thy soul-impassioned fire
                    Possest!

She comes! and speaketh one by one
The names of Haydn, Mendelssohn,
                    Mozart;
Beethoven too, and many more,
But that of Handel gleameth o'er
                    Her heart, —

In golden letters deftly spun
Upon her robe. " My darling son ! "
                    She cries ;
And, pointing to his simple name,
Her smile of joy, Love's sacred flame
                    Outvies.

To him whom charming Music owns
As dearest, greatest of her sons,
                    Outbreathed
Be homage mine, and fondest praise !
Be Handel's brow with laureate bays
                    Enwreathed !

THE CHILDREN OF THE STONES.

Thro' the great city the people haste,
Guided by circumstance to and fro,—
Threading their way thro' the crowded streets,
Hither and thither, for weal or woe :
And, 'mid the din of the motley throng,
Pity is pleading in plaintive tones,
For those unfortunate waifs and strays,—
The homeless children of the stones !

See the young creatures with shoeless feet,—
Each in a network of patches laid,—
Starving with hunger, and wan with cold,—
Under yon archway's inclement shade !

See how they start up in fevered dreams,
Hark to the piteous, feeble moans
Issuing out of the pallid lips
Of those poor children of the stones!

See them again, in yon dingy court,—
Deep in the cellar's pernicious gloom,—
Huddled together,—unwashed, unfed,—
Buried by Want in a living tomb!
Oh, let your hearts be attuned for those
Whom fickle Fortune thus oft disowns,
And lend a willing right hand to aid
The wretched children of the stones!

What mournful pages the lives of these!—
Pages of history traced in tears;
Lives of old age at the gate of youth,—
Cycles of time in a few sad years!
Cradled in crime, and unloved, untaught,
Naught for their pettiest crime atones;
Tho' begging a crust of bread had saved
Those starving children of the stones!

Men of the world! Oh, let Love subdue,
Your sinful and heartless vanity;

Remember that these poor waifs belong
To our common, base humanity !
And let your hearts be disposed to love, —
Your hands to aid,—those whom no one owns,
Those naked and hungry,—homeless strays,—
The helpless children of the stones !

Think of them dead in a wealthy land !—
Dead of starvation !   While others lie
Pillowed in Luxury's downy lap,
Smiling, content, as the starving die !
Why should they starve in a Christian land
When selfish and opulent social drones
While away Life in a golden dream ?
God help the children of the stones !

How can one look on those wasted forms,—
The sickly gaze,—and those scalding tears ;—
The tiny face stamped with Hunger's crest,—
The pleading look which each visage wears,—
And fail to feel the benignant glow
Of Love,—whom Heaven in love enthrones
In all our hearts,—moving each to aid –
The friendless children of the stones !

Young in their lives,—in their hearts how old !
Blighted by Poverty's blasting breath,

For them are none of the charms of Life,—
For them is the peaceful sleep of Death!
Dead? What a God-sent deliverance!
Little they care where they lay their bones!
Angels have wafted their souls above,—
God loves the children of the stones!

'NEATH THE LINDENS' SHADE.

THE spot that is greenest and freshest to-day
In Memory's landscape of life-scenes gone by,
Is the village where childhood's sweet dreams glided
    past
Like a young sunbeam's smile o'er the face of the
    sky.
Methinks, now I gaze on the fast - flowing
    stream,
On whose banks, ah! how oft, with my school-
    mates I've played,—
I see the old church with its ivy-clad porch,
And the haunt we loved best, 'neath the lindens'
    soft shade.

'Twas there, in my boyhood, the chords of my
    heart
First awoke to Life's purposeful beauty and bliss;—
'Twas there in youth's noon-day that Love's holy
    spell
Was breathed o'er my soul by affection's first kiss.
When Summer's warm breath thrilled each tremu-
    lous leaf,
And the wayside by Flora's fair hand was arrayed,—
With bosom attuned to the music of love,—
Oh ! how oft have I sat 'neath the lindens' soft
    shade !

Once more Fancy paints that loved home of my
    youth,
And fond recollection illumines each scene,
While Life's saddened eve is made happy and gay
When I think how unclouded the morning has been.
Ere the flickering spark of existence has flown,
My last wish will be near that spot to be laid,
Which is brightest to-day, in the vale of the past,—
Where my soul smiled so oft, 'neath the lindens'
    soft shade !

TO ——— .

(ON THE DEATH OF HER MOTHER.)

PERHAPS we should not sorrow when the autumn
  leaves are falling,
When the sap which fed the foliage is returning to
  the soil,
But, when the voice of Heaven to a human soul is
  calling,
We dread the ruthless shaft of Death which naught
  on earth can foil.

And when his barb has sunk within the bosom of a
  mother,
Whose love has girt her children like the tendrils of
  the vine,
Their very souls are weeping, and they try in vain
  to smother
The flood of tears which gushes through each desolated shrine.

Then Memory, ever fondly, her mantle folds around
  them,
And breathes a softer halo o'er the ruin Death has
  wrought;
While Hope renews the links upon the silken chain
  which bound them,
And hallows their affection in the labyrinths of
  Thought.

Ah! none may call the loved one back, once passed
  through Death's dark portal,
Or lure the gentle spirit from her blissful seat
  above,
Or feel again that sacred glow,—though earthly, yet
  immortal,—
The bright unclouded sunshine gleaming from a
  mother's love.

The loss we mourn, alas! how great! a mother
  tender-hearted,
The idol of her children, and the radiance of her
  home;
But they shall meet again who now by cruel Death
  are parted,
Where, folded in "Our Father's" arms,—no death
  can ever come!

—

Unfading reminiscences are round me fondly
    stealing,
Which, ever fresh and beautiful, in Memory's land-
    scape bloom;
And thus a youthful poet pleads, with every tender
    feeling,
To cull a wreath of simple flowers, and lay them on
    her tomb!

THE KEEPER'S COTTAGE.

THE Keeper's Cottage stands alone,
Beneath the tinted, leafy shade
Of Fernleigh's tall, ancestral trees;
And, bosomed in a mossy glade,
Where wildflowers bloom, and brackens
    wave,—
Sweet song-birds carol overhead,
And, crooning ever, onward flows,
The brooklet o'er its pebbly bed.

Around the porch wisteria hangs
In rich festoons, while roses blend
With fragrant jasmine's pallid bloom,
And, love-locked thus, their shelter lend

To form a bower which overlooks
A little garden flanked with yews,
With tasteful care arranged, and stocked
With simple flowers of varied hues.

The hale old keeper and his wife
And only child here live content;
And Fernleigh's lovely, sylvan scenes
Have no more graceful ornament
Than this lone cottage, deftly placed
By Art in Nature's fair retreat,—
An Eden-like abode, wherein
True, trusting hearts responsive beat.

Here Love holds court, and pious worth
Goes hand in hand with honest toil,
And hourly duties, hourly wrought,
Crown Life's probationary moil
With hallowed benisons; unknown
The hollow world's beguiling arts;—
Unfelt its envy, pride, and guilt,
In trusting souls, and faithful hearts.

Each morning brings the smile of health
To speed the glowing streams of life
Through bosoms cheerful and serene,
Yet eager for the daily strife:

And evening sees them sit around
The table spread with wholesome fare,—
Commune in twilight's sacred hour,
And close the day with praise and prayer.

Oh! home of Peace,—abode of Love,—
Untainted by the breath of Vice,
· Could aught in human form assail
The charms which make thee Paradise?
Lives there the wretch in manly shape
Who dare pollute the sacred spot
Where Piety and Worth reside
With Love and Virtue,—though a cot?

THE ROSE AND FLEUR DE LIS.

THERE is no flower, in sunny bower
              Which grows,
For beauty rare, that can compare
              With dear old England's Rose.
Fond Summer's breath its sweetness fills,
The poet's soul its beauty thrills,
And, from its bosom, it distils
              The power of love:

The hallowed emblem of our land,
By Heaven placed in Freedom's hand,
When Britain's charter, heaven-planned,
    Came from above;—
'Beloved by every patriot soul
    In whom pride glows,
It blooms to deck our glory-roll,—
    The envy of our foes!

Young zephyrs woo a lily blue,
    With glee,
Upon whose breast the sunbeams rest—
    The lovely Fleur de Lis!
She opes her soft cerulean eye,
Which vies with heaven's canopy,
And bends to greet each passer-by
    With charming grace:
The oriflamme in many a fight,
Where Freedom strove with tyrant Might,—
Where Justice battled for the right,
    And shrieked for place,—
Upon her pale, transparent cheek
    The dew-drops dance;—
With queenly brow, and beauty meek,
    She smiles—the hope of France!

Oh! may those flowers in peaceful bowers
Still bloom!
May Justice pour her sunshine o'er
Oppression's direful gloom!
Long may old England's standard wave,
The glorious ensign of the brave!
And may our Rose, which Heaven gave
At Freedom's birth,
Adorn its kingdom by the sea,
The talisman of liberty!
For ever may its mission be
A blessing upon earth:—
The honour-crowned escutcheon of
The great and good;—
The power to bind all hearts in love,
And Christian brotherhood!

THE DELL.

THERE is a spot,—I know it well,—
Where fairy elves and wood-nymphs dwell,
A sweet, secluded, flowery dell,—
The haunt of childhood;

'Twas there I wooed fair Annabel,
And there I first heard Philomel
Enliven with her dulcet swell
                    The waving wildwood.

Methinks I hear the music still,
As, stealing from the laughing rill
Which sported through its heart at will
                    In softest numbers,

It ecstasied affection's thrill:
I sip the nectar bees distil
From primrose, thyme, and daffodil,
                    Where Beauty slumbers.

Again upon its mossy side
I seem to rest at eventide,
And see the golden sunbeams hide
                    In purple glory;

And there,—as Dryads round me glide,
With Love's soft glow beatified,—
I breathe again in hopeful pride
                    The old, old story.

Oh ! dear to me is that green dell,
Where daisy, thyme, and heather-bell,—
The violet, may, and pimpernel,
        Love's dream sustaineth ;

And ever round my heart shall dwell,
Its softly-stealing, love-fraught spell,
Which Life's rude blast can never quell
        While memory reigneth !

SONG.

FAREWELL ! I cannot bid thee stay
When Duty calls thee far away ;
        Yet, when beyond the sea,—
Though Honour's wreath may crown thy brow,
And Fortune's smiles thy name endow,—
        Oh ! sometimes think of me!

Though fairer forms may court thy smile,—
Though brighter eyes thy heart beguile,
        And brightest beam for thee, —
Oh ! let some memories of home
Within thy glowing bosom come,
        And sometimes think of me.

And oh! should cherished hopes depart,
Which erst have gleamed within thy heart,
　　　　　And sorrow sadden thee,—
Oh! then,—in such an hour as this,—
Remember my fond parting kiss,
　　　　　And, dearest, think of me.

Should sickness pale the blush of health,
Or Fortune fail to give thee wealth,
　　　　　And bowed thy spirit be,
Let bygone days, in memory shrined,
Come stealing gently o'er thy mind,
　　　　　And sometimes think of me.

Should faithless friends thy trust betray,
Or hope-born day-dreams melt away,
　　　　　And dark thy prospect be;
Whate'er may be thy future lot,
Oh! dearest one, forget me not,
　　　　　But sometimes think of me.

While Life within this bosom glows,—
Whate'er the future may disclose,
　　　　　This heart thine own shall be;
Then let sweet memories oft move
Within thy breast the power of love,
　　　　　And sometimes think of me.

NEMESIS.

HAD I a foe implacable, whose hate
Had stung me deeper than my soul could bear,
And filled my being with a fell revenge,—
I would not plunge a poniard in his breast,
Or mix some subtle potion in his cup,
Or yet proclaim him vile, unto the world ;
But I would kindle in his inmost heart
Consuming, inextinguishable Love,—
Love unrequited, hopeless, vehement,
Fed and intensified by mad Despair ;—
Then laugh to see him, day by day, decline,
The frenzied victim of a quenchless flame,
Which scorched and blasted every thread of life,
Yet would not hasten on the end besought.
And, when the ceaseless flow of burning thought
Rolled incandescent waves of molten fire
Into the chamber of his heart and brain,—
When Reason shook, and agonising pangs
Had well-nigh made a chaos of his mind,
And wrung his writhing spirit on the rack
Of ruthless jealousy ;—I would present
The unrelenting object of his love
Before his hollow, passion-lighted eyes,

And fix his gaze upon her worshipped form
Clasped in a rival's passionate embrace;—
Would let him see the face he idolised
Grow dark with scorn, and scowl at his approach,
Without a tear of pity or regret,
Without a smile to soothe his raging breast,—
The hand he longed to kiss in reverence
Point him contemptuously beyond her doors :
Then let him hear the music of her voice,—
Now dissonant with anger and disdain,—
Bid him begone in words of scathing ire,
And strain its sweetest notes to call him "Fool!"
Thence, in his footsteps, I would follow on,
And mark the crisis of his wretchedness :—
The pallid brow, and hectic, sunken cheeks,—
The trembling gait, and shrunken wasting form,
In which the springs of life were almost dry,—
Nor pause until the ruin was complete,
And Death, at last, in pity had released
The broken spirit,—from the world removed
A luckless mortal, and to earth consigned
Another victim to the power of love !
Could mortal mind more retribution seek,
Or human hate exact more full revenge ?

BE TRUE TO THYSELF!

" This above all, to thine own self be true,
And it must follow, as the night the day,
Thou canst not then be false to any man."
Hamlet, Act 1, Sc. 2.

THERE'S a proper time for everything beneath the
shining sun,
Yet the path of duty each of us should tread,
There's a battle to be fought,—there's a swift race
to be run,
So when Duty gives the signal, go ahead!
But to realise success there's a secret that I know
Far better than the thirst for power or pelf,—
Though you travel with a friend, or must struggle
with a foe,
In Life's pilgrimage,—be faithful to yourself!·
Then be true to yourself, whate'er may betide,
And you cannot be false to your neighbour;
Self-respect is the truest and best stamp of pride,
Self-reliance will sweeten your labour!

When your hopes seem overshadowed, and, with
    hearts and minds depressed,
Your trials seem too difficult to bear,
Still on Providence rely, and resolve to do your best,
And remember *work* will drive away *despair!*
If a friend seems going down the hill, prevent him
    if you can,
And do to him as you would be done by,
But be righteous in yourself when you chide your
    fellow-man,
Then you may hope to help him when you try.
    Then be true to yourself, whate'er may betide, &c.

If your toil and worth at length have gained the
    recompense you sought,
Be just, while you are generous to all;   [thought,
In a frank and honest breast, cherish no unmanly
Nor permit your mind to change at every call.
Bear in mind that selfish hearts hold no fellowship
    with those
Who with independent worth have aught to do,
So, without a selfish thought,—whether Life gives
    weal or woes,—
Be faithful to yourself and neighbour too!
    Then be true to yourself, whate'er may betide, &c.

A THOUGHT.

I SAT beside the margin of a stream,
In pensive, but refreshing solitude,
And, fancy-pinioned, in a noon-day dream,
I thought of Life,—its evils, and its good.

I looked upon the water's smiling face,
I saw the sunbeams glitter on its breast,
And heard the music of its gladsomeness,—
Its sweetly-plaintive murmur of unrest.

I saw the Summer rain-drops sink within
The liquid bosom of the crystal flood,
And so, I thought, the mind of youth draws in
The germs of evil, or the seed of good.

They fall into the chambers of the soul
Like circling rain-drops in the restless stream,
And darkly spread, as gloomy night-waves roll,
Or coruscate in Wisdom's hallowed gleam.

I peer within the blue, transparent deep,
And see the pebbles strewn upon its bed;—
I see the meshes of the lichens creep
Around them, like a mantle o'er the dead.

I

And such, I thought, seem unfulfilled desires,—
Hope-stars extinguished in the breasts of men;
The wrecks of that ambition which aspires
To things unknown—beyond all human ken:—

Our good intentions; whose parhelion light
Lures with a fitful and ephemeral gleam,
Then steeps our lives in dark oblivion's night,
And sinks our hopes as pebbles in life's stream.

*   *   *   *   *

The undercurrents' of the quickened soul,
Must flow o'er depths with human passions rife;
O'er dank, dark tarns of human nature roll,
And flood the mighty ocean-bed of life.

Then shall the mortal, through the eye of faith,
His title read to immortality;
Then shall love's life, triumphant over death,
Love's faith reward with love's reality!

A SEASONABLE APPEAL.

Our island-home lies bounden in the grasp
Of ruthless Winter; and his icy hand
Has stricken deep the dwellings of the poor:

With paralysing power his freezing breath
Curdles the life-rills in the people's hearts ;
Want frowns, and stalks triumphant thro' the
    land,
And, in his train, Despair, Disease, and Death,
With fiendish joy, obey his fell behests,
While golden hands alone can loose the cords
Which bind our poorer brethren to the wheels
Of unrelenting Poverty, and crush
Their blighted, withered hearts with cruel strength.
How many homes around us now are drear,
And bare, and comfortless ! How many souls
Are drooping now in hunger-smitten forms,
Which shiver in the scanty, tattered rags
Of dire distress ; without a fire to warm ;
Without the bare necessities of life ;
The parents' hearts with silent anguish wrung,—
The sickly children crying out for food !
O men of Wealth ! this is a time to prove
The texture of your hearts,—your gratitude
For all the benisons on you conferred !
O men, my brothers ! Leave the shrine of Self
And stretch your hands out to these starving ones
Within a stone-throw of your happy hearths !
Open the purses which " Our Father" hath
In loving kindness for you amply filled,

And help our honest and deserving poor,
Our needy brethren,—for we all are His !
Think how they suffer,—what they must endure,—
The pangs of hunger, misery, and cold,—
No smile to cheer, no hope to bear them on ;—
(Unless that certain hope beyond the grave !)
Their little circle pining, mayhap thinned
By sateless death, or prostrate with disease,
And yet all this unmerited by crime !
Think of the children,—powerless to express
The aches and pains which waste their little forms
And wear their lives away, because grim Want
With monstrous hands has touched the mother's
    breast
And dried the streams of the maternal fount !
Oh ! suffer not those feeble little souls,—
Whose lives are sacred to their parents' love,
Who foster love, and whom our Saviour loves,—
To pass uncared for from the earth away ;
To fade like flowers in Poverty's rough grasp,
To die from hunger when your tables groan ;
To die unaided when you might have saved,—
And mount as angels to the throne of God,
Recording there your inhumanity,—
Your base ingratitude and selfishness,   ·
Alike to Heaven, and your fellow-men !

Law visits with a vengeance swift and sure
Each known infringement of her many codes,
(Thank God that poverty is not a crime !) ,
Yet Justice, oftentimes, has turned away
In scorn and anger from her austere Courts !
And yet the poor are human ; and when Want
Has almost maddened them with gaunt despair—
When the foundations of their honesty,
(How many sieges they have stood God wots !)
At length begin to yield, and not a hand
Is feelingly outstretched to bear them up,—
Is it a wonder that the Tempter's voice
At last prevails, and the poor victim falls
Amid the ruins of that hallowed fane
Which a fond mother helped him to uprear ?
Thank God that Britain venerates the shrine
Of Truth and Virtue! and her daughters still
Command the homage of the good and brave,
The love of saints, the fealty of the world !
Yet God's most fair, most perfect handiwork,—
Exposed to dread adversity, and left
Unhelped, unpitied, to pursue her way
Thro' Life's rude scenes,—temptations manifold ;
Forlorn and helpless, hungry, destitute
Of home or friendship, and her graceful form
Draped in the scanty raiment of distress —

May be assailed by some inhuman wretch
Who prostitutes the sacred name of Love;
And, with the shimmer of his rank and gold,—
With wiling arts, and specious promises,
Wakes Love's pure passion in her own pure heart,
And, when her soul is prostrate at his feet,
Effects her ruin,—leaves her to despair,
To sink still deeper in the depths of sin,
While he, unpunished, passes gaily on,
Caressed by Fortune, and by Fashion wooed!
A little help, a kindly-spoken word,
Might have secured her from the doom of guilt,
Might have preserved her poor young soul from
     shame;
But ruined now, alas! And yet more poor,—
Still left to battle with the Tempter's snares,—
Ah! who dare follow in her downward course,
Or gaze, unmoved, upon her dismal end?
Oh! kindly hearts, and sympathising minds,
Think not,—because the sorrow-burdened poor
Are ever with us, that they have no worth,
No honesty, no virtue in their souls;
Strive not to make a crime of poverty!
Nor yet, because a few, more sorely tried,
Or gifted with but feeble moral strength,
Have yielded to temptation in their pangs,—

Consider all, alike, to be despised!
The poor alone know what they *must* endure,
How they are tempted, and how sad their fate!
Oh! then, my brothers, let both hearts and hands
Be zealous in the service of the weak,
The poor and needy; think, oh! think of Him —
Our Great Redeemer—Whose Divine commands,
Whose earnest prayers, and faithful promises,
Were ever manifold in their behalf:
Whose precious Word entreats us above all
To glorify our God: to live in peace,
Fraternal love, and Christian charity.
And when, as yet unwritten, history
Shall tell of Britain's greatness and her power,—
When ages, yet unborn, shall con with pride
The valour of her sons, her daughters' worth,—
Brighter and brighter may her glory-roll
Blazon before the nations of the earth
Her deeds of Love and Charity: and writ
In golden letters on the page of Truth,
May men admire this witness to her name—
" She fed the hungry; loved and helped the poor! "

UP AND BE DOING.*

It is useless to mope o'er our troubles all day,
And to rail at the lot we inherit;
Bear in mind that success is the crown of hard
    work,
And we all receive more than we merit.
Though the past has been dark,—though the present
    is drear,
And a storm o'er the future be brewing,
Bright sunshine will smile, ere a very long while,
If you only be up and be doing!   [man,
    Then get up with the lark, and to work like a
    The dictates of conscience pursuing,
    And, to o'ercome the strife in the battle of Life,
    Never yield, but be up and be doing!

Never think it beneath you to dirty your hands
If Duty require you, but do it,
For however humble a duty may be,
If righteous, you never can rue it.

---

* Published by Hopwood & Crewe.

As you steadily plod o'er Life's dangerous road,
The chart of the past keep reviewing,
Yet, while you look back o'er the desolate track,
Still keep travelling on, and be doing!
    Then get up with the lark, &c.

The drop that is constant will wear out the stone,
So, if Fortune be slow to reward you,
Be cheerful and patient, and toil on in hope,
And your conscience, approving, will guard you.
Make hay while the sun of your youth brightly
    shines,
Or else all your life you'll be rueing
The time you have spent, and the chances you've
    lost,
So don't fret, but be up and be doing!
    Then get up with the lark, &c.

THE OLD CHAISE.

SINCE poets have sung of their " Old Arm Chairs,"
" The Old Wooden Bucket," and " Clock on the
    Stairs,"
May I not be permitted to rhyme in the praise
Of a time-honoured relic,—our dear old chaise?

Its wheels have long perished, its springs are
    decayed,
But its body still rests in our garden's fair shade,
In a flower-kirtled corner, with beeches o'erspread,
And the rose and convolvulus wreathed round its
    head.

Behind is a lane with soft clover o'ergrown,
And each window looks out on a scene of its own,—
The garden, the orchard, the fragrant hedgerow,
And the beautiful daisy-gemmed valley below.
With the sun's golden smile o'er the cherished old
    thing,
And the birds perched above while they joyously
    sing,—
While round it the honey-bee sportively plays,
There's no fairer arbour than our dear old chaise.

Its cushions are tarnished, and faded its lace,
And deadened the hues of its tawny old face,
Yet there's grandeur which boasts bygone riches
    and pride,
In the gold-stamped morocco which decks its
    inside.
The trappings of ancestry hang on it still,
Recalling the past with fond memory's thrill,

While the bright coat-of-arms on each panel dis-
    plays
The noble descent of our cherished old chaise.

And now in our garden the old thing is laid,
And we love to recline in its sweet peaceful shade;
While oft in the twilight we sit there and sing,
Or list to the bells as for vespers they ring ;
Or breathe vows of love as they steal from each
    breast,
As the day-god in splendour declines in the West ;
For love-tales are whispered, and sung Love's
    sweet lays
In the peaceful retreat of our cozy old chaise.

Oh ! if it could speak, what a tale it could tell
Of Hope's trembling birth, and Affection's mute
    spell ; —   [shrine,
How Love has held court in that hallowed old
And ruled o'er true hearts with a sceptre benign.
Oh ! sweet are the silent charms round it which
    cling,
And dear every nook of that honoured old thing,
And while memory back o'er the past fondly strays,
We'll cherish with pride our beloved old chaise.

WEE WILLIE.

OH! weep not, youthful mother, though the
  floweret of your love
Has been taken from your bosom in its early-
  oping bloom;
In Heaven's fadeless arbours, angels cherish it
  above,
Then why shed unavailing tears beside an earthly
  tomb?

The perfume of your tender little blossom now is
  blent
With the amaranthine fragrance breathing through
  Elysian bowers;
Then, wherefore mourn the tiny bud for which the
  Master sent,
That it might bloom eternally amongst His choicest
  flowers?

Oh! weep not, lonely mother! for the precious
  babe who smiled,
And nestled in your fond embrace is with the
  angels now:

Look up!—beyond earth's boundaries, and see your
    darling child;—
The glory in his infant face,—the name upon his
    brow!

There, with the seraph-hosts of God who sweep
    the golden lyres,
And sing the song of the Redeemed around the
    Father's throne!
See! 'mid the glory-burst of Love which never-
    more expires,
Your little one an angel there!—God's angel, yet
    your own!

Oh, mourning father! murmur not, or deem life
    sad and drear,
Because your heart is desolate since little Willie
    died;
However dark the night may be, the sun will re-
    appear,
And Heaven's richest blessings are but trials
    sanctified.

Oh, doubt not, stricken mother! Though your
    loved one is no more,—
Though your soul is crushed and drooping, and
    your cross is hard to bear;

Have faith, brave heart! Your darling is "not
   lost but gone before,"
And, in the mansions of the blest, awaits your
   coming there.

Seek not to know the purposes of God's mysterious
   will,
But bow in meek submission to Love's chastening
   decree;
Think not that God has promised what He will not
   yet fulfil,
And, in the plans of Providence, the Hand of
   Mercy see.

Weep not! Rejoice, oh, chastened ones! The
   angel-hosts of God
Rejoiced to see your baby-boy from earth's temptations won;
With resignation bow to kiss the love-afflicting
   rod,
And, looking up to Heaven, pray, "Oh, God! thy
   will be done!"

THE SUN WILL SHINE AGAIN.

THERE is no lot so cast
In sorrow's tear-stained mould,
But has some ray of hope
To cheer with joy untold;
Then yield not to despair,
Tho' duty goads with pain,
And all is dark around;—
The sun will shine again!

If earth were free from care,
And all was peace within,
Whence, then, the worth of life
In triumphing o'er sin ?
Where faith and truth unite,
A blessing will remain;
Then labour on in hope,—
The sun will shine again !

When Nature's gloom prevails,
And Winter dims the view,—
When all seems sere and dead,
'Tis but to live anew!
Then courage ! Though your cup
Life's bitter dregs contain,
In it are gems dissolved,—
The sun will shine again !

The good and bad on earth
For wisest ends are given,—
To try our simple faith,
And make us meet for Heaven ;
Then trust in Providence,
Toil on, with might and main,
And, drear though all may seem,—
The sun will shine again !

Life is an April day,
A spring of joy and sorrow ;
Sunshine and showers to-day,—
Smiles and tears to-morrow !
So, let contentment still
Within our bosoms reign,
And, though our way be dark, --
The sun will shine again !

The seed must perish first,
Which is to bloom anon ;
So, care must purify
To lead us heavenward on ;
Then, whatsoe'er our lot,
From idleness refrain ;
Work, and trust Providence,—
The sun will shine again !

SPRING WILD FLOWERS.

—•o>•(o•——

" Even weeds the chief,
May have drops of honey."
FRANCIS DAVIS.

K

IMPROMPTU LINES.

(IN ANSWER TO A QUESTION.)

"WHERE I most like to be" depends
On circumstances, I aver,
But with my tried and trusty friends,
I'm always happy anywhere!

If sad, I'd be where I might sip
The flood of sympathy which rolls,
In gentle waves of fellowship,
From loving hearts, and cheerful souls.

If merry, I would like to be
With those I love, and with them share
The essence of my mirthful glee,
Distilled without a drop of care.

I like to be where crystal streams
Meander thro' the waving woods, —
Where Fancy's beatific dreams
Enliven Nature's solitudes.

As joy supreme, be mine to woo,—
When moon and stars keep watch above
The sylvan shades we wander through,—
The graceful form of her I love !

GO IN TO WIN !

Life is a battle-field,
Faith is a sword and shield,
None e'er but cowards yield,—
    Warring with sin ;
Comrades ! the foe is nigh,
Seek valour from on high,
On, then, to do or die !
    Go in to win !

Firm in each strong right hand
Grasp virtue's quenchless brand ;
Be of good courage ; stand
    Firm 'midst the din ;
Let the shout loudly rise,
" On, for the victor's prize,
Danger and death despise,
    Forward ! to win ! "

Scorning sin's bondage-yoke,
Strike, as one felling stroke,
And, 'mid the clang and smoke,
    Plunge boldly in :
Battling for God and Right,
Trusting in Heaven's might,
Be heroes in the fight,—
    Go in to win !

Be our souls overcast
With hardships falling fast,
Be ruin sweeping past,
    Never give in :
Toil all the harder then,
If you fail, try again,
Plunge in the strife like men,—
    Go in to win !

Struggle with might and main,
Ever the Right maintain,
Passion and self restrain,
    Yield not to sin ;
Tho' Life's rude cares oppress,
Tho' doubts and fears distress,
God will each trial bless,—
    Go in to win !

Never of aught afraid,
Never by Fate dismayed,
Seek gracious Heaven's aid
    Ere you begin ;
On, then, for Truth and Right,—
Duty your chief delight,
All heroes in the fight !—
    Go in to win !

HOMEWARD BOUND.

GLADNESS thrills the sailor's bosom,
And his heart is full of glee,
For this is a day of sunshine
In his life upon the sea :

And he works with quickened vigour
As he hears the welcome sound
Of his captain's voice, exclaiming
" Ready, men ! we're homeward bound ! "

Soldiers who, afar off fighting,
For their country and their Queen,
Have withstood the battle's fury
Where Death busiest hath been,—
Now exult, with hearts uplifted,
And mirth quickly spreads around,
As the bugle, sounded loudly,
Loudly echoes " Homeward Bound ! "

Christian-pilgrims in Life's noon-day,
Armed with truthfulness and faith,
Plunge within the raging battle,—
Fondly court the eve of death !
Well they know the gory conflict
Shall with victory be crowned,
And with fearlessness remember
They are heavenward, homeward bound !

Brother, on Life's stormy ocean,
Comrade, in Life's bivouac,
Hath the gleam of Faith illumed you
Into Virtue's hallowed track ?
Up, then : fear not in the struggle,
Love's fond arms our souls surround,
Heaven smiles upon our journey,—
We are onward, homeward bound !

Hope and joy illume each bosom,
Gladness reigns in every breast,
Years of toil, and care, and trial
Soon shall merit hallowed rest.
Mercy's beacon-light is burning,
Let the air with joy resound,
Soon we'll reach " the better country,"—
We are onward, homeward bound !

Let us hasten on our journey
In a brotherhood of love,—
Help our weaker fellow-pilgrims,
And their doubts and fears remove :
Tho' upon Life's rugged highway
Mighty barriers be found,
Let our hearts be cheered by feeling
We are homeward, heavenward bound !

FAREWELL.

As morning diffuses her aureate light
O'er Nature's luxuriant carpet of green,
Our deepening friendship affection became,
Our hearts were united,—our hope-star serene.

We loved, oh, how fondly! with what deep
    devotion
We breathed to each other those soul-stirring
    words,—
" As one, and for ever, whate'er may betide us,
We'll bask in the sunshine which fond love affords."

Oh! sweet was the dream from which now we
    awaken
To realise Cupid, Fate's menial at heart,—
Our hearts disunited,—our hope-star extinguished:
The phantom has vanished, and now we must part!

But yet,—tho' on this side the grave we are parted,
And ne'er more will follow in hope's luring train,—
There is a fair haven, where, once we have
    entered,—
Where once we have met, we shall ne'er part
    again.

Oh! Mary, 'tis hard thus to part, and for ever,
And think of the days that will never return ;—
When Love shed around us a halo of promise,
And caused our fond hearts with affection to burn.

Now tears dim my eyes, as I think yet I see thee
As once thou wert near,—but unweaved is the spell
Which bound us so fondly, alas! but to sever;
And now, may God bless you! Dear Mary,—
　　Farewell!

A PASSING KNELL.

NEAT, tho' dressed in a well-worn garb,
With her golden hair unkempt and free,
A maiden hastens with timorous step
To toil for the scions of "high degree."

Who could depict that fair, young face,
Pallid and anxious from grief and care,
But beautiful still in its girlish prime,
Tho' Sorrow has moulded her impress there?

The heavenly blue of her April eyes,—
Intensified by her soul's pure gleam,—
Like the moon o'erspreading a placid lake
With the chastened light of her silvery beam,—

Suffuses her face with a pensive smile
Which softly over each feature plays;
While her exquisite mouth, and lofty brow
Would have charmed the heart of Praxiteles!

Who is this maid with the lovely face,
The chaste, sad look, and the faded dress,
Wending her way thro' the crowded streets?
Alas! but a poor young governess!

Once she was happy, and rich, and gay,
As arch and as coy as a cushat dove,—
Her parents' idol,—the sunshine of home,
Diffusing around her a halo of love:

Now,—Oh! Misfortune hath ruthless been,
And Death hath her fondest hopes o'erthrown,—
Bereft that young soul of home's hallowed joys,
And left her in poverty,—friendless, alone!

'Mid the din and the tumult of Life, alone!
With scarcely a smile to lighten despair,—
With waning strength, and a breaking heart,—
Yet daily she toils for her scanty fare.

Poverty, hunger, or sickness, or all
May prostrate the form of the poor young maid,
And thus she may starve, and starving, die;
But even of Death she is not afraid,—

For the "still small voice" of her simple faith
Whispers within, "In Heaven there's rest,"
And, murmuring not at her Father's will,
She longs to repose on her Saviour's breast.

* * * * *

Oh, Fashion! Oh, Riches! Oh, heart of man!
Divine retribution shall come with power!
Think of her thrown in a pauper's grave,
Without one mourner to cast in a flower!

The underpaid slave of the worldly great,—
Wise, accomplished, beautiful, good,—
She died of starvation,—want, neglect,
When wealth ran riot thro' gentle blood!

"Ashes to ashes, and dust to dust,"
Throw in the clods o'er the pauper's shell,
And leave the clay in its kindred earth;—
The Spirit has gone with her God to dwell!

"Ashes to ashes, and dust to dust,"
While unseen angels a requiem sing;
"Only a governess !" So saith the world !
"Died of starvation !" Poor, young thing !

LET'S BE CONTENT.

Life has its sunshine as well as its sorrow,
And unto all of us talents are lent ;
The cares of to-day will seem blessings to-mor-
    row,
Whatever our lot, then, oh, let's be content !

Tho' Hope's horizon is fraught with obscurity
And Life's vicissitudes make us lament,
If we act nobly, God is our surety
That we shall prosper, so let's be content !

Every cloud has a bright silver lining,—
A halo of promise which to us is sent ;
Dark tho' to-day be, with sunny hopes shining
To-morrow may dawn ; oh, then, let's be content !

Tho' expectations, desires fondly cherished,—
Our fervent heart-yearnings be trodden and rent,—
Tho' the sweet bouquet of Life may have faded,
Still strive with courage, and let's be content!

God doth but try us as chivalric warriors
Tested their swords, until broken or bent;
Mercies are shrined up in Life's greatest barriers,
So, be submissive, and let's be content!

Work with a will, then, and labour in earnest,
Toil on in love ere our days are nigh spent,
And, when the chastening hand seemeth sternest,
Trust still in Providence,—let's be content!

Tho' some less worthy may drink Life's suc-
cesses,
And our dreary lot a sad contrast present,
Be of good courage! their recompense less is
Than our's, if we're faithful, so, let's be content!

Whate'er betide us in sunshine or sorrowing,
To Hope's sweet "still, small voice" ever consent,
Bright rays of promise from Faith's lustre borrowing,
Ever trust Providence,—let's be content!

CHIDE SOFTLY.

LET a fellow-feeling warm you,
Let sweet mercy temper law ;
Light, itself, has spots of darkness,—
Soundest metal has its flaw.
Sin is human : softly chide then,
Ever speak in loving tone ;
Other's faults reprove in kindness,
Censuring as you would your own !

Solace dark despair with mercy,—
Soft words bend the stubborn will,—
Lighting up the soul's dark chambers,
And the hardest heart will thrill.
Softly chide, then ; let affection
Speak to those whom you condemn,
Let love be the hallowed blessing
That will fructify in them.

Shed the glow of pure affection
O'er the souls of those you blame,
For, however drear the spirit,
Love can kindle virtue's flame.

Words of kindness ne'er are wasted,
Speak them gently where you may,—
Pearl-seed sown by passing angels
O'er Life's rugged, weary way.

As the sunshine woos the zephyr,
Let the sunshine of your love
Beam within the evil-haunted
Soul of him whom you reprove;
Softly chide in words of kindness,
With love draw the erring back,
Leading them from error's darkness
Into Virtue's radiant track.

THERE'S A CORNER FOR LOVE IN EVERY HEART.

IN the gloomiest cell there's a pencil of light,
In the depths of despair there's a glimmer of hope;
There's a halo of promise,—a planet of peace
Set in Destiny's dreariest horoscope.

Oh, then, say not that all Life's affections are false,
Or that Life's tears and trials no blessings impart,
While our Father hath hallowed with fatherly care
Love's inviolate altar in every heart!

When old Winter has breathed upon fair Nature's
    face,
And has bound her in ice-moulded shackles asleep,—
When the storm-king stalks over earth's paralysed
    breast,
And the furies brood over the billowy deep;
Oh, 'tis only that Nature in life-giving Spring,
From her torpor, with increase of beauty may start;
And e'en thus, though our souls may be sin-bound
    and drear,
There's a corner for Love kept in every heart!

There's a leaven for evil,—a leaven for good
At perpetual strife in humanity's breast;
And the purpose of life is the triumph of good
Over evil;—the bane of the purest and best.
Let us fearlessly follow the pathway of Right,
As portrayed upon Duty's infallible chart,
Keeping onward and upward : and Truth will illume
Love's own consecrate corner in every heart!

If misfortune, or poverty, doubt, or despair
Should embitter our life-cup, and make us forget
That our faith is being tested for merciful ends,
Why should hope be subdued by inactive regret?
To repine is unworthy; be zealous, be strong;
And profane not your manhood by time-serving art,
But, persistently toiling and trusting, still strive
To diffuse Love's warm sunshine through every
    heart!

Oh, despise not the outcast who, friendless and
    shunned,
Is abandoned to fate, unregarded, alone!
And remember that he who is sinless and pure
Has alone any warrant to throw the first stone!
Seek to quicken the virtue-germs still left within,
And with gentleness urge him from vice to depart;
Oh! attune those soft chords on affection's sweet
    lyre,
Which awake Love's own music in every heart!

Oh! then, judge not in wrath; still in kindness
    reprove,
Nor seek ever to hasten a weak brother's fall;
Bear in mind that the *best* of us nothing can boast,
And must answer for sin to the Father of all!

L

Oh! then, speak to the erring in mercy's sweet tones,
Let affection the counsels of virtue impart;
And however or oft a weak brother may fall,
Ne'er forget that Love hallows a place in each heart!

USE THE OTHER HAND!

A LITTLE boy a wheel was turning,—
  Turned with ceaseless toil,—
On a rope-walk I was passing,
  Strewn with many a coil;
I asked him what he did when tired
  Turning wheel and band,
And he smilingly replied, "I
      Use my other hand!"

In this world we all must struggle,
  If we wish to live;
Cares will fly, and troubles vanish
  If we only strive.
Let each plod in honest labour,
  Bearing Virtue's brand,
And, if tired, we must only
      Use the other hand!

Here, below, we're placed on trial ;
  We have gifts to use ;
Work to do, and strength to do it,
  Why should we refuse ?
Though our hopes are dashed to pieces
  On Life's rocky strand,—
And our spirits sink within us,—
      Use the other hand !

If the burden of our sorrow
  Crush our hearts with woe,
As if they must cease for ever
  With each poignant throe:
Let us pray for strength to bear it,—
  Prayer's a magic wand ;
God will help us if we struggle,—
      Use the other hand !

By small strokes, and oft-repeated,
  Mighty oaks are felled ;
Let us humbly ask, and patience
  Will not be withheld.
If success crown our endeavours,
  And our sails are fanned
O'er Life's tide by worth and labour,—
      Use the other hand !

Let us help our fellow-worker,—
    Help his load to bear;—
Cheer him on with words of kindness,—
    Smooth his brow from care:
Let the harvest of our efforts
    Make our hearts expand,—
Clothe the poor, and feed the hungry,—
        Use the other hand !

Success we never can inherit,
    There's no royal road !
Honest toil and noble conduct
    Win the smile of God !
Let us, then, be each determined
    Trials to withstand ;
Trust in God, love man, and labour !—
        Use the other hand !

THE IRISH MAID.*

In that fair sea-girt isle, where the shamrock grows
On its velvety, emerald sod,—

---

* These lines, embodying the fiction of a school-boy, were written at an early age, and are inserted without alteration.

That rich gem of earth which Nature loves most,—
Where she smiles thro' the soul to God;—
Where streams measure music, and sea-waves sing
    wild,
Where the young sunbeams sport thro' the glade;—
Where soft balmy breezes above whisper peace,—
I first met my dear Irish maid.

The morning was young, and the ambient air
Was fraught with the warblings of Spring,
While a flood of sweet song from feathery throats
Made the pale azure welkin ring:
The bright purple orient, flecked with gold,
Had kissed away every shade
From a mossy dell where the wood-nymphs dwell,
And there sat my fair Irish maid.

In wonder I gazed, but my loud-throbbing heart
Must have told her a stranger was nigh,
For, raising her head, then blushing, she smiled,
And saluted me timidly:
Weaving a wreath from the flowers at her feet,
And her exquisite form displayed,
A spell was entwined round my rapturous soul
By that beautiful Irish maid.

Her lovely young face, with its fond beaming smile,
Was scarce like a creature of earth,
And the halo of purity 'circling her brow,
Almost spoke of her heavenly birth.
As I held her fair hand, I sighed as I thought
That a being so pure must fade
Like the garland she wove, which I lovingly placed
On the brow of that dear Irish maid.

Like dew-drops embalmed in the lily's pale breast,
With a rose to keep watch on each cheek,
Her eyes, dark and dreamy, looked forth from her soul,
Of the treasure there hidden to speak.
And as love's gentle voice whispered hope to my
O'ercome by emotion I prayed   [heart,
That I might be permitted o'er Life's shifting sands
To succour that sweet Irish maid.

Her soft ebon hair, by the zephyr set free,
Flowed gently o'er shoulders as white
As the silvery moon, when erst she went forth
To kiss the calm bosom of night.
Like an angel divine, by God sent to earth,
Selfish man for his sins to upbraid,
Truth's guileless simplicity beamed in the smile
Of that chaste little Irish maid.

The daisies looked proud to be kissed by her feet,
And the primroses lifted their heads
To gaze on her form, while the violets breathed
The fragrance of morn from their beds.
As she walked by my side in that bliss-yielding
    hour,
In her meek, native graces arrayed,
The bouquet of beauty no flower had more rare
Than my coy little Irish maid.

Oh, Erin ! Fair country of verdure and song,
Purest gem in the casket of earth,
Long, long may thy daughters be cherished by
    fame
For beauty, and virtue, and mirth !
May thy sons in their choice be as happy as I,
When from that fairy arbour I strayed
With my arm round the waist of my *colleen dhas*
    dhu
My own darling Irish maid !

DARBY'S LAMENT.

Och! the joy of my heart has departed for ever,
And life to me now is both dreary and lone,
Since Norah, my colleen, has crossed the big ocean,
And from dear ould Erin in sorrow has gone.

Oh, pale was her brow on that pitiless mornin',
Her lovely soft eyes were half-blinded with tears ;
And her fair bosom heaved with the storm of
    emotion,
As she thought of the home she was leaving for
    years.

Yes, may be for ever ! She's left all behind her,
Her friends and her counthry she ne'er more may
    see,
But, colleen agra,' sure while life beats within me,
I'll still love you true, tho' heart-broken I be.

When I think how we gambol'd in innocent child-
    hood,
Among the green fields of our own beloved isle ;—

When we heard the birds sing, and the streams
    murmur music,—
How happy the hours that we thus did beguile!—

When I think how the time rolled on bright and
    unclouded,
How she lived in my bosom, asleep or awake,—
How the friendship of years burst out into affec-
    tion,—
There's no joy for me, and this poor heart must
    break!

I can never forget the fond smile that she gave me,
As, clasped in my arms, she sobbed out her "fare-
    well,"
Oh, while memory lasts it will haunt and support
    me,
And sleep in my soul like the holiest spell.

Och! Norah, acushla! tho' waves roll between us,
And you may now pine on a far distant shore,
Your Darby is true, and while life lasts will love
    you,
Tho' he ne'er may embrace you, or gaze on you
    more.

I'm desolate now, since by fond hope forsaken,
My spirit is broken and bowed down with care;
When I think how the sun of my life has de-
    parted,
Och ! sure, 'tis a load that is heavy to bear.

May heaven surround you with love, Norah darlin',
With friends that are gentle, devoted, and kind,
And should a harsh word ever pain you, mavourneen,
Oh ! think of poor Darby in grief left behind.

All the luck and the blessin' has left the ould
    counthry,
There's nothin' but hardship and crime in the
    land ;
And now that you're gone, love, I've nothin' to
    care for,
And I, too, must sail for the foreigner's strand.

Och ! you will not forget me, my own Norah
    darlin',
Sure, tho' I am poor I am honest and true,
And heaven may yet send down some of its sun-
    shine
To gladden the heart of your Darby and you !

I'll work for you, darlin', in love and devotion,
Sure, may be, our partin' was all for the best,
And when Fortune smiles on my labours, achora,
I'll clasp you for ever with joy to my breast.

     *   *   *   *   *

Dear ould Erin! Of Nature's fair handmaids the
    fairest,
'Tis sad that your sons from their green sod must
    roam,—
That tears should be shed in the land of the stranger,
When joy should have reigned in each bosom at
    home.

Oh, what is the raison your sons and your daughters
Can't live in the land where their forefathers dwelt?
Why should grim Discontent plant the apple of
    Discord?
There's room for us all whether Saxon or Celt!

Farewell, now, sweet land! And may peace and
    contentment
Smile on you once more, as they did at your birth;
And may Erin yet gleam from the breast of the
    ocean,
The favoured of heaven,—the pride of the earth!

May virtue and truth still distinguish your daughters,
May your sons both in valour and wisdom excel,
May the spirits of peace, love, and hope dwell
within you,
Dear, ould land of my fathers! Dear Erin! Farewell!

SONNET.

(ON BEING ASKED BY A LADY " WHO IS YOUR FAVOURITE POET ? ")

WHERE all are fair, 'tis difficult to choose
The fairest blossom from a choice bouquet,—
Where all are beautiful how hard to say
Which is the sweetest,—which has richest hues?
So with the poets;—each delightful muse
Bestows some grace on gentle Poesy;
Yet, to select a single flower or lay,
Which owneth charms supreme, I must refuse.
While Moore and Milton, Shakespeare, Burns and
Scott,—
Byron and Tennyson, are Britain's pride,

To institute comparisons is not
The way to honour those by none outvied !
Be this, then, lady, my reply to you,—
I love all flowers,—and love all poets, too !

————

LA VERTU EST LA SEULE NOBLESSE ! *

THAT the blue-tinted blood of the worldly-great,—.
Though the river has flowed from a Norman sea,—
Proves the loftiest rank in the scale of worth,
Is the vilest and shallowest sophistry.
It is false !   Although Fashion has lent her aid
To conceal the romance with her arch *finesse*,
'Tis the record of Heaven,—the law of Truth,
La vertu est la seule noblesse !

Oh, then prate not to me of escutcheons pure,
Which have never been sullied by stain or slur,
Even Art will not sanction what Nature scorns,
Nor withhold her debasing *bend sinister*,

————

* These lines were written at a very early age.   The
author can no longer justify the spirit in which they
were written, while admitting the justness of the motto.

Though voluminous pedigrees grace the halls
Of the Fortune-befriended,—and may impress
The weak minds of a few,—yet, despite them all,
La vertu est la seule noblesse !

Let his lordship rejoice in his garish joys,
And exult in his title and wealth : in ease
Let my lady in Luxury's lap repose,   [grees :
While they both boast their time-honoured pedi-
But the virtuous only are truly great !
And the poorest, though drooping from dire distress,
May be worthier far than those dons of earth,—
La vertu est la seule noblesse !

Tho' the good things of earth on a few are showered,
While the others have little but toil and care,
Yet the blessings of Heaven descend on all,
And the poorest e'en more than the rich may share.
For the heart is the fountain of real worth,
As the mind is the standard of manliness,
And, despite rank and riches, 'tis Truth proclaims
La vertu est la seule noblesse !

Oh, then, give me a man,—be he e'er so poor,
With a leal, honest heart, and contented mind ;—
Who is manly, yet gentle ;—forbearing, just,
And is true to his God,—to himself, and kind:

Such, alone, are the worthily, justly great!
Who, tho' trials and dangers around them press,
Can be faithful to death, and trust all to God !—
La vertu est la seule noblesse !

Oh, then, let the possessors of rank and wealth
Rest assured in their pride, and their riches scan,
He is nobler and richer whom God inspires
With the meek, simple faith of an honest man !
In the high court of Manhood, he ranks as one
Whom the Noble of nobles delights to bless,
So, despite riches, titles, and all beside,
La vertu est la seule noblesse !

PSYCHE TO TELLUS.

WHEN Heaven on Creation's morn,
Proclaimed the advent of thy birth,
Archangels kissed the newly-born,
And angels welcomed thee, oh, Earth !
Then thou wert innocent and fair,
And, nestled at the breast of Love,
The founts of Virtue fed thee there,
While cherubim kept watch above.

Thus cherished and caressed beside
Thy gentle foster-brother Time,
The years primeval onward glide
Till o'er thee gleamed youth's golden prime ;
Then Nature sped to deck thy brow
With vernal wreath, and fragrant flowers,
While, at thy feet, her handmaids bow,
And scatter gifts in lavish showers :
And Music, floating, from above
On seraphs' wings, her voice to raise,
Charmed thy immortal mother, Love,
And swelled an anthem in thy praise.
Successive cycles, eddying round,
Deepen the blush of maidenhood,
And Heaven's courts with joy resound.
As Deity proclaims thee " good " !
When Time, reclining at thy feet,
Salutes thee as his virgin bride,
And Love and Truth the union greet,
While Nature smiles, beatified.
Then, for a season, holy Peace
Presides within thy bowers, oh, Earth !
And Heaven's mystic labours cease,
In honour of thy first-born's birth ;
From thine Almighty Maker's throne,
With Life's eternal mystery,

To consecrate, as Heaven's own,
Thy children, I came down to thee,—
And, shedding glory's quenchless ray,
The "form divine" with beauty shone,—
Gleamed with a soul the moulded clay,
Which God had stamped His image on!
Thus were thy sons ordained to wear
The semblance of thy God above,
And destined with Himself to share
The sempiternity of Love!
Came, then, the Tempter in disguise,
To test thy primal offspring's faith,—
To prove them innocent and wise,
Or seal their doom with sin and death.
And this in love:—a Father's care
Revealed in the Creator's plan!—
His jealous nature to declare,—
His fond solicitude for man.
They fell, oh, Earth! And Eden's bloom
Was shrouded in the pall of Death;
And Nature, steeped in Sin's dire gloom,
Bewailed the fate of perjured faith.
Ages rolled on: yet, evil-fraught,
They ope thy gates to Sin's dark flood,—
The glorious works which Heaven wrought,
Sink down to depths where demons' brood,

M

And those immortal souls which glowed
With God's own image, ere beguiled,
Commingle, in the fell abode
Of Satan, and the sin-defiled.
The breath of hate, by furies blown
O'er Nature's Paradise, inspires
Thy erring children to enthrone,
Within their breast, those fierce desires
Which urge to fratricidal strife,
And sow the seed of endless woe,—
Call forth fell passions into life,
And plan at Heaven's overthrow.
Thus, with the ages, deeper dye
Imbued the sin-bound souls of men,
Till Mercy saw with pitying eye,
And Love sent Hope to thee again :
And God to men is reconciled
By sending His own Son to them,
When, on the Eastern sages smiled
The holy star of Bethlehem !
Earth ! thou art old and wrinkled now,
Yet Love and Mercy compass thee :
Still Nature decks thy tawny brow,
And cheers thee with her melody :
Time's waning ocean onward rolls,
Yet Sin stalks o'er thy flowery sod ;

Oh! influence thy children's souls
To look through Nature up to God!
Soon I must wing my upward flight,
And Time shall from his throne be hurled;
And I, from Love's eternal height,
Shall weep o'er a dissolving world!
Let not sweet Mercy call in vain,
Oh! hear the pleading voice of Love!
Let Truth and Peace together reign,
Ere I am called from thee above.
Let Faith inspire thy sons to trust
A Saviour's all-atoning blood,
Ere dust regain its kindred dust,
And Heaven dries up Mercy's flood!
Then shall Millennium's hallowed dawn
Burst through thy gloom in glorious rays,
And all thy nations shall be drawn
By God, to share His mysteries!

CPSIA information can be obtained at www.ICGtesting.com
Printed in the USA
BVOW08s1021100714

358767BV00025B/589/P